STAFF SUPERVISION IN THE PROBATION SERVICE

Staff Supervision in the Probation Service
Keeping Pace with Change

MICHAEL DAVIES
Senior Probation Officer
Derbyshire Probation Service

Avebury

Aldershot · Brookfield USA · Hong Kong · Singapore · Sydney

Published by
Avebury
Gower Publishing Company Limited
Gower House, Croft Road
Aldershot
Hants GU11 3HR, England

Gower Publishing Company
Old Post Road
Brookfield
Vermont 05036, USA

British Library Cataloguing in Publication Data

Davies, Michael, 1946–
    Staff supervision in the probation service:
    keeping pace with change.
    1. Probation services — Great Britain —
    Personnel management 2. Supervision of
    employees
    I. Title
    364.63'068'3   HV9345.A5

Library of Congress Cataloging-in-Publication Data

Davies, Michael, 1946–
    Staff supervision in the probation service:
    keeping pace with change / Michael Davies.
        p.   cm.
    Bibliography: p.
    Includes index.
    ISBN 0-566-05623-2
    1. Probation officers — Great Britain.
    2. Supervision of employees. 3. Corrections —
    Great Britain — Administration.
    I. Title.
    HV9345.A5D38 1988
    354. 410084'93 — dc 19   87-35906 CIP

ISBN 0 566 05623 2

Printed and bound in Great Britain by
Athanaeum Press Limited, Newcastle upon Tyne

Contents

Acknowledgements

This book stems from a piece of research undertaken as part of a masters degree in Social Services Management, at Lancaster University. I would like to thank the staff of the social administration department at Lancaster for their expertise and encouragement. Particular thanks go to Professor Tutt and Professor Hadley, Dr Janet Finch, Senior Lecturer Susan Clayton, and last but by no means least, Dr Ben Shapiro for his assistance with computer programming.

I must also thank Derbyshire Probation Service for substantial support in a variety of ways. The committee, senior management and field staff have all been very generous in their support.

Thanks also to my wife and children for not complaining about lost weekends, and finally to Linda, my secretary, who often transformed untidy scrawling into something understandable.

MSc Social Services Management abstract

The probation service has developed rapidly throughout this century, particularly during the last thirty years. Task and practice have widened considerably and continue to do so. However, the practice of staff supervision within the service does not seem to be keeping pace with change. By far the most popular style adopted across all grades is the supervisor working with six or seven supervisees on a one-to-one basis with occasional group meetings thrown in.

This piece of research strives to assess the nature of supervisory processes within the service and their effectiveness.

The history of staff supervision is traced, including the role of magistrates, the Home Office and supervisory grades. The impact of developing professional practice is also considered in an attempt to understand how the current situation has been reached.

The views of probation officers, seniors and assistant chief officers have been researched regarding the purpose, practice and effect of supervisory processes within the service.

Lastly, a review of work currently being undertaken within services on this subject has been carried out which may be helpful to those in the service dissatisfied with their present system but finding it difficult to develop a more appropriate process.

1 An introduction

The supervision of staff in the probation service has always been and will probably continue to be a contentious issue. When supervision of staff was first formally introduced to the service nearly seventy years ago the debate concerned the simple issue 'should probation officers receive supervision?'. Recent studies demonstrate clearly that this is no longer an issue in the Service. There is broad acceptance at all levels that supervision is necessary. Most would go further than that and say that from a management perspective supervision is vital if services are to monitor accurately what is happening within their organisation and ensure that an acceptable level of service delivery is being offered to those we serve. From a fieldworker perspective most would say that supervision is vital to good professional development and that field workers have a right to expect good quality supervision of their work to be provided by management.

Why then does the topic of staff supervision still raise such strong emotions within the probation service? Simply in my view, because there is little agreement on the what, when, how, why and who of staff supervision.

(a) What should be supervised?
(b) When should supervision take place?
(c) How should supervision be carried out?
(d) Why be supervised, what are the objectives?
(e) Who should supervise who?

We should not be surprised that we have not yet resolved these issues. Let us not forget that we are still struggling to find the right balance of care and control with our clients, why therefore should we be surprised that these two elements also cause us problems when related to the supervision of staff?

The aforementioned is of course a very simplistic view of the problems attached to staff supervision. Our difficulties have been made much more complex over the years due to the rapid change and expansion that has taken place within the service, particularly in the last thirty years. As the service's range of tasks has expanded so has the service itself in terms of personnel. This has meant that a range of new tasks has been given to supervisors under the broad umbrella of staff supervision. The growth of specialisation, project development, the need for improved information systems, resource managing, staff evaluation and many other developments all carry implications for staff supervision which if not adequately addressed will at best confuse all concerned regarding the purpose of supervision. At worst they can create tensions which are both disabling for supervisors and those they supervise.

Perhaps the most challenging development concerning staff supervision in the 1980s is the Home Office statement of National Objectives and Priorities.[1] For the first time service management has been given a framework within which to produce its own local Statement of Objectives and Priorities. Obviously these statements must be monitored within services and some assessment made of progress towards the stated ends. Periodically these objectives and priorities must be reviewed. This provides management with an opportunity to focus supervision more on tasks and targets and to move away from the more personalised supervision that has characterised service personnel management for decades. However, there are snags. Not everybody will agree with the Home Office statement and/or their own local Statement of Objectives and Priorities. Whilst not wanting to suggest anarchy be condoned it is important that management provide opportunities for staff to comment on the likely effect of various policy initiatives on their clients and the feasibility of suggestions coming from above. Over-emphasis on prioritising and target-setting, backed up by a narrow approach to supervision, could harm the much needed exchange of views required at all levels within the service if policy decisions are to be soundly based. The buck of course stops at the doorstep of our clients who suffer from a poorer quality of service if supervision in the broadest sense is not effective.

The words 'staff supervision' have been used several times in the preceding paragraphs. The author's understanding of staff supervision in the probation service may be different from that of the readers.

Discussions with senior probation officers, for example, suggest strongly that what they view as 'good staff supervision' will reflect their years of experience in the post and when they were trained. The new breed of senior probation officers is encouraged to see itself as resource managers, and in terms of staff supervision this could well mean introducing a range of supervisory models aimed at persuading their team to share experiences and knowledge to the benefit of all. The longer-serving senior probation officers have developed skills as casework consultants and see their supervisory role as encouraging officers to meet in a safe atmosphere on a one-to-one basis to discuss their work in a constructively critical manner. However, neither of these approaches appears to place much emphasis on the vitally important area of accountability. Research on this topic suggests there is overwhelming agreement that all staff in the service should be accountable to someone. This will normally be a line manager. Timidity regarding the nature of this accountability can result in the accountability component of staff supervision becoming a 'hidden agenda' item. Statements of National and Local Objectives and Priorities are likely to bring issues of accountability more sharply into focus and this may be no bad thing. Many people in the service may find they are being asked to be more specific about their objectives and priorities and how their contribution fits in with service needs. They are aware that progress should be checked and periodically reviewed. Much of this will take place under the banner of staff supervision, thus we find staff at all levels requiring information regarding the objectives and priorities of the supervisory process itself. What is it for and how should it be applied?

A working party in 1984, set up by the East Midlands branch of the National Association of Probation Officers, was given the task of enquiring into the state of staff supervision within the East Midlands area. The working party had been convened in an atmosphere of considerable alarm following the dismissal of a probation officer of many years standing. It is not appropriate to dwell on that incident, except to say the quality of supervision offered to the officer prior to his dismissal became an issue. Other probation officers were asking themselves if a similar fate could befall them if they were unlucky enough to be in the wrong place at the wrong time.

The working party looked at supervision within the area and produced a report which was helpful to the general debate about the future of staff supervision in the service.[2] One of the recommendations was that a conference on the topic should be arranged. A positive step at this point was that East Midlands chief probation officers committed time and money to the conference. Each county in the region agreed to send staff at all levels to the conference, and a chief probation officer joined the conference planning group. In the autumn of 1985 the conference was held and feedback suggested it had achieved its primary objective, getting staff supervision 'out of the closet'.

This book builds on the start made at the 1985 conference. The original objective was to review the supervision of probation teams and consider models of supervision which might assist teams towards their stated objectives and priorities. It seemed likely that as the range of tasks the service was expected to undertake grew, as practice developed, as specialisms emerged, all probation teams would need to review their supervisory processes. A phrase used as the basis of much of the author's early thinking comes from Payne and Scott's work on supervision in fieldwork teams: 'Every team should develop a supervision scheme, which will be unique'.[3] However, it soon became obvious that this would be impossible without first taking a wider view. There was insufficient hard information regarding the purpose and nature of supervision in the service generally to focus specifically on 'How to do it in the 80s'. Therefore a review of objectives was needed. The review of objectives drew largely from the National Association of Probation Officers' working party and the conference planning group. It also included some work with a group of experienced probation officers looking at needs and aspirations. This review led to the production of a lengthy list of issues:

1   What are the objectives of supervision?
2   What effect does the service personal evaluation process have on staff supervision? All staff have periodic evaluations written on them by managers which are very important documents in terms of career prospects. These documents are supposed to be the basis of ongoing work between supervisor and supervisee. However, many staff comment that they are often forgotten documents that suddenly become very powerful when an application for promotion is made and a reference is called for. How 'safe' is it therefore to engage in frank, open discussions with supervisors if they are periodically making these assessments? Is the evaluation process an aid to good supervision or does it distort the process?
3   As the service expands more specialisms are emerging. For example the service involvement in civil work appears to be rapidly moving towards the category of 'specialist activity'. The growth of day care is another area in which we now have many people with specialist expertise often unfamiliar to line managers. Do specialists have special needs? How should they be supervised? Often specialists do not fit into the line management system very

4

well. For example research and information staff often have specialist knowledge with a whole county to service. What model will best provide them with support and guidance whilst also ensuring everybody is clear and happy regarding line management accountability?

4   Roles within the service are changing. Probation service assistants are no longer merely back up to officers. Often they are now recruited for specific skills, expertise or experience they have which the service needs. For example probation community service assistants that become project managers. The role of officers is placing more emphasis on their role as broker, guiding clients towards opportunities to improve their quality of life, as opposed to individualised counselling focusing on the individual. This suggests that whilst officers may be using their traditional casework skills in a small number of cases, in the majority they are acting as a manager, bringing the client into contact with a range of service, and/or community resources.

Senior probation officers are increasingly becoming resource managers with the added responsibility of initiating projects within teams or the community if the need is there. Requests to produce initiatives may come from management or field staff and these requests must be prioritised and worked on with the resources available. Decisions on these requests and the priority given to them must make sense above and below if progress is to be made.

As the service grows it becomes increasingly unrealistic for chief officer grades to have their fingers on the pulse in all areas and issues. Acting as 'senior senior' and 'doing the rounds' on a weekly or monthly basis is likely to result in the criticism that management does not initiate, placing undue emphasis on controlling. However, as chief officers 'let go' in order to concentrate on service development they can then be accused of living in an ivory tower and thus not in a position to realistically play a part in staff supervision. All staff need to increase their understanding of changing roles within the service but this does raise the question 'who should supervise who?'.

5   What will the long term effects of little or no growth in the service during the 1980s be? Whilst task and practice have continued to change rapidly the size of the work-force has not. However, it is right to say that those entering the service in recent years have been mostly better qualified than even a decade ago. Thus we are moving towards a situation in which we have a growing number of young, highly motivated, well qualified staff, growing in experience with few opportunities for promotion.

Michael Willson commented on this in an interesting article in 1984. He observed that staff are blocked from promotion by the cessation of recruitment and that they have limited scope for the expression of their skills. Thus the problem becomes 'What can we do about the frustration of our officers and how can we work with them to allow everyone to benefit from their ever increasing experience and expertise?'[4] This situation is likely to lead to higher expectations from staff concerning the supervision they receive and if we do not positively respond to this call we run the risk of having a large number of disillusioned, apathetic, perhaps cynical staff within our service.

6 We regularly hear about the rapidly changing task and practice within the service. What precisely does this mean and what are the implications for staff supervision?

7 What are the training needs of supervisors? How are they assessed? How do we ensure that relevant courses are provided for supervisors? At present there are compulsory courses for new senior and new chief officer grades but after that training becomes vague and will often depend on the enthusiasm of managers themselves. Is this inevitable? Are there other ways in which the training needs of managers can be addressed?

8 Recording supervision. Is it good practice for an agreement regarding the recording of supervision to be drawn up? What are the expectations regarding the content of supervision records? Who should do it, who should see it, when should entries be made, why record at all?

9 What is the nature of this beast called staff supervision? Is there any agreement regarding the essential elements? It is often said that good supervision should be a combination of support, professional development opportunities, monitoring and accountability issues. Is there more to it than that? Are these elements compatible? Can they be separated and tackled in different ways?

10 It could be argued that the assessment aspect of supervision is the easy part. It is only when the assessment is completed and the conclusion is that the supervisee's work is unsatisfactory that life gets difficult for everybody. What happens or should happen when this point is reached? What should the supervisor's response be? What is the supervisee entitled to expect in terms of support to reach a satisfactory level? When and how are the difficult decisions made?

11 Are models of supervision negotiable? If so how should these negotiations take place and who should be involved? It is expected that service managements would wish to ratify all

models suggested by teams or managers. What are the implications of this for managements?

12 Much of staff supervision is based on an assumption that there are agreed standards of practice. To what extent is this true? Is it desirable to put more effort into the setting of standards within the service? Some services now have extensive practice manuals that lay down in great detail practice guidelines. How can standards/expectations of professional practice be set and who should be involved in this process?

13 Is there any link between the quantity and quality of supervision? How can quality be assessed?

14 Should we take more care of officers at particular points in careers? It seems generally accepted that first year officers should receive special attention but what about the problems of 'burn out' after the first few years, the needs of the very experienced officer with more than ten years still to serve, the officer in poor health, or those nearing retirement?

This list of issues, much overlapping and some contradictory, proved extremely awkward to embrace with concise objectives for this book. The author focused on four logical steps which could act as a framework, thus the four objectives eventually became:

1 *To review the development of staff supervision in the probation service.*

2 *To obtain the views of staff as to the current purpose and nature of staff supervision in the service.*

The views obtained will be at three levels within the service: chief officer grades, senior probation officer and probation officer. Particular attention will be given to:

(a) The process of supervision.
(b) What are the appropriate relationships? Who should supervise who?
(c) What are the different components of the supervisory exercise?
(d) What are the perceived objectives?
(e) What effect does supervision have?
(f) How do those involved feel about the process?

3 *To explore the likely effects of recent developments in service task and practice on staff supervision.*

Whilst other issues emerge, particular attention is given to considering:

(a) The growing emphasis on working with 'high risk' offenders in the community.
(b) The growth of project work within the service (e.g. day care, tracking schemes, reparation schemes).
(c) The changing and developing roles of staff at all levels.
(d) The trend towards developing 'packages' within probation orders that commit clients and staff to tighter contracts with courts than the basic probation order.
(e) The movement towards teamwork approaches to tasks, observable in many parts of the country.
(f) The influence of local Statements of Objectives and Priorities.
(g) The development of specialists and specialisms within the service.

4   *To consider the varying demands made of the supervisory process and explore models of supervision that may assist the service in its efforts to improve the quality of service delivery.*

Notes

1   *Statement of National Aims and Objectives* — Home Office, 1983.
2   *Report of Working Party on Supervision*, NAPO (East Midlands Branch) 1984.
3   Payne and Scott, *Developing Supervision of Teams in Field and Residential Social Work, Part I*, NISW paper no. 12, 1982.
4   Willson, M., 'Management retention and control of skilled, sophisticated staff in the late '80s', *Probation Journal*, vol. 31, no. 1, March 1984.

2 The history and development of staff supervision in the probation service

The difficulties we are encountering at present regarding staff supervision are not new; indeed a historical glance back within the service suggests that many of the problems we are still struggling with have their roots embedded in service history. For example the issue was the subject of debate with Home Office officials, magistrates and probation officers within three years of the service being launched in England and Wales in 1907. Dorothy Bochel notes a conversation between Canon Barnett of Toynbee Hall and the Home Secretary that took place within a few months of the introduction of the probation system in England and Wales. She states that Canon Barnett

> suggested the appointment of superintendent probation officers. The Canon feared that magistrates might fail to give sufficient attention to the choice of officers for each case. A superintendent with a good knowledge of the various officers under him would be able to advise the magistrates on this point and could also be used as an inspector of the work done. The chief metropolitan magistrate was told that if he or any of his colleagues wished to experiment with such an arrangement the Home Office was willing to make the appointment. The chief metropolitan magistrate thought it best to begin on simplist lines.[1]

Here we have, at the very beginning of the service's development, the first signs of the tensions that would last decades, concerning who owns the service, and to whom should it be accountable?

It seems right to say that the first supervisors provided for the service were magistrates. The Home Office signalled its acknowledgement of this prior to 1907 when there was considerable debate as to the qualities required to be a probation officer. During these debates there was a strong lobby for the existing police court missionaries to be handed the role of probation officers on the grounds that they already had considerable experience of courts. Some felt retired policemen would make good probation officers whilst another body of opinion felt that recruitment should be from 'the higher classes' who would adopt the role of 'educators'.[2] After many years of debate the Home Office decision was that local magistrates could make their own decisions as to the type of person they appointed. At this stage supervision of probation officers' work had not evolved, but clearly magistrates were being offered control, in a broad sense, of the development of the service.

During the next few years there was considerable growth within the service and with it complaints about service organisation and further requests for a supervisory grade. A government committee set up to review progress in 1909 concluded that supervisory grades were not needed as:

(a) The volume of work was insufficient.
(b) It would weaken the responsibilities of officers and restrict the individuality of his/her approach.
(c) Magistrates would lose track of individual probationers.

The committee seemed anxious that the service should not distance itself from courts and were clearly concerned that supervisory grades could reduce the important links between individual probation officers and magistrates.

> The committee of 1909 saw close links with courts as advantageous. The link in fact was not only that between employer and employee but between co workers in the task of dealing with offenders.[3]

The 1909 committee were also well aware of the need to promote the use of probation in courts if this infant service was to grow and felt strongly that magistrates should have 'an encouraging role' in the development of the service. Their report stated:

> There could be no greater encouragement to probation officers and no more potent means of contributing to the success of the probation system than for the magistrates themselves to show interest in their work.[4]

Thus we can see that in a relatively short space of time, approximately three years, the service had turned to magistrates regarding the qualities needed to be a probation officer, workload control and allocation, inspection of individual cases and general encouragement and support for their work.

During the next few years the service began to develop its credibility under the eye of local magistrates. However, the notion of a supervisory grade did not go away and was highlighted in 1914 when the first book devoted to probation work in the United Kingdom was published. Cecil Leeson's *The Probation System* suggested a special Home Office unit with peripatetic supervisors. Further, he suggested the introduction of principal probation officers who would be accountable to a committee of local magistrates.[5] It seems Leeson's thinking was a little ahead of his time and the Home Office response to these suggestions via Home Office circulars reaffirmed that 'the responsibility for probation work lay with the magistrates themselves'.[6]

In 1920 a Home Office departmental committee chaired by Sir John Baird considered yet again the possibility of a supervisory grade but decided against the idea, preferring to 'leave development in local hands'.[7] However it did suggest the Home Office share the cost of running the probation service on a '50/50' basis with local areas. Whilst it seems reasonable to assume that local areas were happy with this suggestion it did require them to put forward schemes for running the probation service. These schemes had to be 'submitted for Home Office approval'.[8] There does seem to be an inconsistency here with local areas being encouraged to develop their own services but needing central government approval. Nevertheless Baird's recommendation is important in that for the first time the Home Office appears to be developing an oversight role regarding the development of the service.

The 1920s saw a gradual increase in workload for the service and commensurate expansion in numbers of officers. This decade also saw two developments which, although they had little effect at the time, became significant a generation later. Firstly in 1925 the Criminal Justice Bill provided for the setting up of 'probation areas' and called for the development of probation committees.[9] In 1926 probation rules were produced which allowed authorities to appoint principal probation officers 'to supervise the work of other probation officers'.[10] However there was considerable anxiety within the magistracy regarding the appointment of principal officers as it was felt that 'the general trend of opinion' was 'against any creation of different ranks of probation officers'.[11] The main fear at that time seemed to be that the introduction of principal officers might interfere with the special and important relationship which should ideally exist between the magistrates, the officers and the probationer.[12]

To summarise staff supervision in the probation service during the first twenty years it could be said that such supervision as there was lay with magistrates, that great importance had been given to the freedom of individual officers and the special relationship between officers and courts, and lastly that there was considerable resistance to the introduction of a supervisory grade. Noises in favour of supervisors came mainly from probation officers themselves but at this stage there seemed no united strong feeling from them on this issue.

As the service work in courts grew over the next few years the cries for a supervisory grade became stronger. This was partly because the probation service as an organisation was growing and the case for managers became stronger simply due to the organisation's size. However, the real strength of the case lay in the fact that the provisions laid down by the 1925 Criminal Justice Act and the 1926 Probation Rules had not been followed up. In 1935 a committee set up to review social work in court heard that:

> 10 years after the Criminal Justice Act 1925 making it mandatory to set up probation committees some areas had not done it.[13]

In other areas there were committees in theory but they had never met! The 1935 committee reported:

> Many probation officers complain they have never met their committee and that they carry out their work without supervision, criticism or encouragement.[14]

The Sussex branch of the National Association of Probation Officers reported that:

> Practice in their area was for the clerk to present the officer's report to the committee. If the officer was summoned to the meeting he usually waited outside the door on the chance that he might be called in to discuss a special case.[15]

The committee found this information disturbing as it clearly suggested there was a lack of direction, order and supervision within the service. They wrote of the need for 'radical changes in the organisation'.[16] In terms of recommendations for the future the social work in courts review produced little new, falling back on Leeson's suggestions, namely that supervision should be exercised through the

Home Office by using inspectors. The role envisaged for these inspectors was not seen as a controlling one. They were to advise, encourage and stimulate those working in the service. The committee also agreed with Leeson that probation areas should have a probation committee responsible overall for the development of the service. To counter the argument that this would reduce the ability of local magistrates to discuss cases with their local probation officer the committee advocated the introduction of local case committees which would adopt the supervisory role. It was said that when a probation officer was in difficulties with a case he/she would be able to turn to the case committee who might be able to 'throw more light on some of his problems', and even 'become a source of strength and inspiration'.[17]

It may be interesting for those of us who are still trying to get the chemistry right regarding probation liaison committees to note that the review committee suggested a probation officer should be secretary to these case committees. It was felt that the Clerk to the Justices should be made, ex-officio, a member of the committee in order that the clerk could 'keep in touch'.[18]

By 1935 the National Association of Probation Officers had been joined by the Magistrates Association in requesting a supervisory grade. The review committee accepted the evidence put forward to further this request and departed from the views of the 1909 Young Offenders committee by suggesting principal probation officers should be appointed to 'supplement the supervisory work of probation committees'.[19] The committee were impressed by the definition of a principal probation officer's task provided by the Glasgow probation committee. This read as follows:

> To advise the probation committee on all technical details of the probation system. To be the executive of the probation committee in the organisation and administration of the system. To supervise field work and all case records of all probation officers in the area.
>
> To act as liaison between the probation committee and the education committee in questions of probation and approved schools, approved homes, remand etc.
>
> To coordinate the activities of the probation department with the police, charitable organisations, social services, clinics, etc.
>
> To encourage by frequent reports and observations the promotion of effective methods for the fullest development of probation.
>
> To arrange the duties of probation officers interested in other forms of social work, that they, fortified and equipped by their probation experience may help such kindred activities; in this way broadening the basis of their social endeavours.[20]

At this stage all concerned saw the introduction of this grade as a positive step and it is perhaps noteworthy that much was made of the principal probation officer role in terms of improving organisational arrangements, developing and encouraging the service. Supervising cases is mentioned but the backcloth of probation officers clamouring for support and encouragement must be remembered. It would appear that accountability issues and individual officers' professional freedom were of secondary importance at this stage.

The 1935 committee also recommended the use of senior probation officers if areas felt there was not a case for a principal probation officer, although the roles and tasks for these two grades do not appear to have differed greatly. However, the important step of establishing a supervisory grade had been taken even if the task and how it could be achieved was a little vague. During the next ten years the principal probation officer role emerged for the most part satisfactorily for all parties but the senior probation officer role was more problematical. The next logical step therefore seemed to be to define senior probation officer duties, and the revised probation rules of 1949 attempted to do this. They suggested the following:

> (i) The duties to be performed by a senior probation officer shall include supervision and advise [sic] upon the work of probation officers, and in particular a senior probation officer shall organize the office work and the distribution of work between probation officers, and examine and advise upon the manner in which they keep their records and the manner in which their working time is used.
>
> (ii) It shall be the duty of a senior probation officer to examine and certify for payment the expense claims of probation officers and the disbursement of and accounting for monies entrusted to them in connection with their duties.[21]

The 1949 probation rules also updated the duties of the principal probation officer but essentially the main tasks of both grades seemed to be improving the organisation's administration and coordinating resources and workload. However the word supervision is contained in the list of duties for both grades and it is important to recognise at this point that the service had been developing, along with social work generally, in terms of professional practice. Consequently the meaning of supervision would have had a different meaning in 1950 to that in 1920. 'Casework' was rapidly gaining ground and supervision in 1950 would not simply mean oversight of workload and duties. The quality of casework was becoming a focus and this would have implications for professional autonomy. To quote Jarvis, commenting on the 1949 Act,

14

The effect of this detailed statement was to establish beyond doubt a hierarchical structure in the service. The sturdy independence of the individual officer had long held sway, and was to do so long after the rules had been issued. But the managerial function of the principal officer and the supervisory duty of the senior officers were now unequivocally stated. As some older officers saw it the glorious days of independent free lancing were over.[22]

During the 1950s the probation service continued to grow, professional practice developed strongly along the individual counselling, 'casework' model and the hierarchical structure Jarvis referred to was consolidated. By 1962 the number of probation areas had been reduced to 103, and sixty-two of these had principal probation officers. Twelve of the sixty-two had senior officers as well. The other areas coped with just senior officers but in all by 1962 there were 158 senior probation officers in post. During this period a new grade was introduced, that of deputy or assistant principal officer. By 1962 there were twenty-one posts of this nature.[23]

The Morison committee set up to review progress in the probation service reported in 1962. Morison recognised the development of service professional practice and the development of the line management system in the service. He stated:

> The supervisory function of both principal and senior probation officers have acquired a new significance as, with the development of casework methods and of understanding of the role and difficulties of the caseworker, appreciation has grown of the help and relief which the probation officer can find in detailed discussion of his cases with a trained supervisor. Such casework supervision requires a high degree of sensitivity and insight and the service is only moving gradually towards its adoption as officers become available who are skilled in modern supervisory techniques. This is a development which must in the future influence the choice of principal and senior probation officers, and the proportion of supervisory posts required.[24]

Morison was clearly moving the supervisory role away from administration to casework consultancy although one of the problems of supervision in our service has been a marked reluctance on anyone's part to allow a responsibility to be shed. The consequence of this has been that as the service has developed, the task of supervision has regularly had new aspects added to it with little being taken away. Thus Morison may well have considered that he was simply adding casework consultancy to the administrative and organisational duties already present. However, the report went on to suggest that recruitment of supervisory grades should reflect the need for skilled casework consultants and these qualities were much sought after in the 1960s which also saw a tremendous growth in the numbers of supervisors in the service. The effects of this situation are still being grappled with today.

Before proceeding further an investigation of the 'casework consultant' role may prove fruitful as this role has had far-reaching effects on the service for approximately thirty years. Firstly, what is casework? I have been in the probation service fourteen years and I still find it necessary to ask for clarification when a colleague uses that term. It probably means something rather different in the 1980s to its meaning in the 1960s, but even in the 1960s there was no universal agreement on the meaning of the term 'social casework'. Furthermore, a whole language was built up around the technique of casework which gave 'caseworkers' a certain mystique which is still present today in some probation offices. Unfortunately as Byrne pointed out, admittedly with the benefit of hindsight, in 1973: 'We had the words but because development [of casework] was so fast there was no agreement on their meaning'.[25]

Byrne's comments on the tendency for caseworkers to develop a language of their own are exemplified by a staff supervisor commenting, 'I am not a teacher, I am a learning facilitator'.[26] Perhaps the nearest we could achieve to agreement as to the meaning and focus of casework in the probation service in the 1960s is the view expressed by Joan King in 1958:

> If behaviour is influenced, often unconsciously, by feeling rather than by rational thought, it is by a change of feeling rather than by rational argument or exhortation that any permanent change in attitudes and behaviour must be sought. If the way people feel about themselves and others is largely determined by their early relationships it may be through new relationships that scars can be healed and a change of feeling achieved. Thus the relationship between caseworker and client, which has always been accepted as a basic factor in giving this kind of individual help, is now seen as of overriding importance. It is recognised as a vital means of healing to be used consciously for the good of the client, whose feelings, hostile as well as friendly can be accepted as an essential part of the process of growth or recovery. In addition an increased awareness of human motivation has thrown light on the reactions of the caseworker as well as of the client. This has given the former a clearer appreciation of his own feelings and of the pressures to which he himself is subject in his relations with his clients. Such feelings, if unrecognised and uncontrolled, may distort and misdirect the relationships, but if accepted cannot merely be controlled but can often be used to enrich the caseworker's understanding and ability to help.[27]

My interpretation of King's description is that the caseworker works with a number of offenders who according to the caseworker's assessment committed their offending as a result of some failing, weakness or inadequacy in themselves as individuals. With the aid of a skilled caseworker, the individual can remedy this malfunction or at least learn to cope with it, and thus offending could be reduced or halted.

If this is what probation officers were doing in the 1950s and 1960s what were the supervisory grades doing with their casework consultant role? Kadushin describes the consultation process as: 'A series of sequential steps taken to achieve some objective through an interpersonal relationship'.[28] However this definition was produced in 1977. If we wish to 'feel' more accurately the role of casework consultant in the 1960s, the following contemporary definition may be more appropriate:

> Professional consultation involves a planned change by which expert knowledge and skills are utilized in a relationship between consultant and consultee (individual group or organization) for the purpose of enabling the consultee to increase, develop, free or modify his knowledge, skills, attitudes and or behaviours towards the solution of a current or anticipated work problem; and secondarily for enabling him to be more effective in preventing or solving similar problems in the future.[29]

The second definition demonstrates the tendency at the time to use jargon which, thankfully, we seem to be reducing in the 1980s. However, it is important to recognise the emergence of this new language in social work as it must have contributed to the confusion regarding the nature of staff supervision in the 1960s.

Returning to the casework consultant role using King and Kadushin's definitions it seems reasonable to suggest that principal and senior officers were being asked to offer non-directive teaching (sorry, learning facilities!) to staff engaged in delicate individual counselling, often long-term, with offenders, with the belief or expectation that clients with improved self-awareness would cease to offend. But how were the supervisory grades to provide this service to the staff? The most popular methods seem to have been borrowed from caseworkers themselves, and in turn some would say caseworkers borrowed much of the casework technique from psychotherapy. I refer to the reflective process. Much has been written about the reflective technique in the supervision of staff although the flood of literature may be subsiding in recent years. If used for supervising staff who are in turn adopting traditional casework methods it may well have much to commend it as a means of developing the supervisee's understanding of his/her clients and the appropriate strategies to employ.

Byrne produced a useful seven-point guide to the reflective process. He refers to trainees but I think his guide stands up when applied to supervisors and workers in the probation service. He suggests:

1   Enable the trainee to define his own problems.
2   Enable the trainee to generate his own problems.
3   Enable him to examine the implications of his own solutions.
4   Enable him to select his own course(s) of action.
5   Never be guilty of offering to the trainee problems which he does not produce himself.
6   Never be guilty of offering to the trainee solutions to his problems.

Or most important of all

7   Never assist him with the working out of his own solutions. [30]

Byrne describes the reflective process fully making it clear that the responsibility for bringing problems out lies with the worker whilst the supervisor should be capable of facilitating in-depth analysis of the client/worker relationship. Janet Mattinson's book, *The Reflection Process in Caseworker Supervision*, may be helpful for those wanting to pursue the technique in more detail.[31]

In my view the problem with the reflective process is that if taken to extreme the supervisor gives nothing to the supervisees who then become resentful and/or defensive. In my view the technique can be dangerous in the hands of an incompetent supervisor who can use it as an excuse for offering no assistance to staff who then become anxious and conservative in their approach. A group of workers faced with such a supervisor can find the reflective technique a block to communication which saps energy and can hold back development. However, this criticism is not of the reflective process itself but of organisations that allow it to be misused by poor supervisors.

Although the Morison report may have suggested a shift of emphasis from administration and inspection to casework consultancy, for supervisory grades in the probation service the administration and inspectorial functions could obviously not be disregarded entirely. This meant that supervisory grades were required to balance these components, not an easy task as there are clear differences between supervision and consultation. The task was made even more difficult by the emphasis Morison placed on the encouraging, supportive role of supervisors with their staff who in turn were struggling with difficult 'casework' issues. The inspectorial and administrative functions appear to be taking second place with

Morison, therefore all concerned presumably found the blurring of supervision with casework consultancy problematical. The most obvious problem is that consultation implies meeting on an ad hoc basis whereas supervision should be continuous. Although provided regularly, consultation cannot be continuous which will in turn affect the issues that can be brought to a consultancy session. Describing the agenda of a consultation Kadushin writes: 'Generally they are, or should be, clearly defined, clearly circumscribed and delimited problems which can be dealt with in a limited period of time'. Going on to point out the essentially voluntaristic nature of consultation he reminds us that it 'Offers the freedom to seek assistance without granting authority to those who give assistance'.[32]

Thus interpretations of Morison's report created confusion as to the role of supervisory grades. Those who wished to hold on to what Jarvis described as 'the glorious days of independent free lancing', would wish to believe that principal and senior officers were there in a consultative capacity with a little bit of encouragement and support thrown in. Those who wished to believe that Morison had validated the shift from magisterial inspection and supervision to professional supervisors in this role could point to Morison's comment that 'supervisory grades had contributed to the quality of the service'[33] and remind interested parties that Morison used the term supervision, not consultation, when considering the duties of supervisory grades. This confusion became even greater in the few years following Morison as the casework technique gained ground. It became standard practice in both social services and probation departments to talk about supervising newly-trained entrants to the service, moving on to consultancy when the officer was confirmed in post and was felt to be an experienced professional. This practice prompted Kadushin to comment:

> The widely accepted suggestion that the relationship between supervisor and supervisee changes gradually to that of consultee and consultant implies that supervisors can, while in their position, relate differently to the worker. It would suggest that at some point the supervisor can set aside the administrative authority and discuss a work related problem with the supervisee now in the role of consultee without any complications of continual worker accountability.[34]

Looking at this clearly I doubt that many probation managements would be prepared to legitimise such arrangements under the heading of staff supervision. Mark Monger acknowledges this difficulty when he describes in detail the supervisor/supervisee relationship with a new probation officer. The new officer has weekly sessions with his senior who 'for the first 2 months or so made no attempt to suggest what the content should be'.[35] The reasons for this are given as possible deficiencies in his basic training which, if there, it is hoped will surface, together with an acknowledgement that the persons concerned do not know each other and the new officer may feel 'unsafe'. I'm not sure that as a new officer I would feel particularly safe having to make the running for the first two months! However, when the officer has settled in the weekly sessions move to helpful case discussions, the cases being picked in such a way to give the senior plenty of opportunity to be encouraging. The new officer is helped to cope with a feeling of rejection by courts when a recommendation is ignored, helped to resist pressure to 'get tough' with a young man and latterly assisted in dealing with workload management issues. Finally the senior moves towards the consultancy model but here Monger is careful to point out the danger of allowing supervision to be completely superseded by consultation.[36] It may be that many of our problems with supervision and accountability issues stem from a lack of clarity in this area.

By 1966, only four years after Morison, concern was being expressed that the role of supervisory grades was still vague and/or confused. At a time when committees were being asked to appoint principal probation officers and senior probation officers primarily for their skills or potential skills as casework consultants, the National Association of Probation Officers were suggesting that duties be reassessed, recommending that organisational and administrative skills be restored to a position of importance for supervisory grades. The National Association of Probation Officers' Working Party had been

> Impressed by the uncertainty in the service about the function and role of senior probation officers and indeed all those who occupy supervisory and administrative posts.[37]

Their report suggested that senior probation officers now had three main areas of responsibility:

(a) Organisation and administration
(b) Casework supervision
(c) Carrying a caseload.

Joan King, in her book *The Probation and After-Care Service*,[38] expanded this suggestion three years later. She felt there were five main components in the senior probation officer role:

1 Direct casework
2 Administration
3 Teaching
4 Consultation
5 Evaluation.

There seems to have been general agreement that the supervisory task contained all the ingredients suggested by the National Association of Probation Officers' Working Party. The debate concerned the balance of the ingredients — should any one of them be more important than the others? King's suggestion that there was an evaluative role was not unanimously agreed. The so-called autonomous probation officer of the 1960s would not have been happy with this suggestion, nor would those who wished to see the probation officer reach fully-fledged professional status. The question of probation officers as autonomous professionals guided by a code of ethics or semi-professionals with supervisors and inspectors is captured by Scott as follows:

> The administrators of bureaucratic organisations attempt to routinize and regulate work in order to assure adherence to minimum legal standards, to obtain equity and continuity of service to clients, and to achieve efficiency of operation and administration. The professional casework staff is usually less than sympathetic to such arguments, questioning the wisdom of many of the legal requirements, protesting procedural regulations and policies which interfere with their discretionary response to the differing problems of individual clients, and willingly sacrificing administrative efficiency in the cause of increased worker autonomy and client service.[39]

Perhaps this debate concerning professional autonomy was part of the National Association of Probation Officers concern regarding the importance being given to the casework consultant role. It might be argued that by using casework consultancy, supervisors could be operating a subtle form of inspection which if attached to a staff assessment role could be quite threatening. The compromise gradually accepted during the 1960s seems to have been that principal officers would undertake the main organisation and evaluative skills whilst seniors would develop casework consultancy and administrative skills.

The development of the principal probation officer and senior probation officer roles allowed the Home Office to suggest that 'It would be a reasonable objective to provide effective casework supervision for all officers'.[40] They asked probation committees to consider a 1:5 ratio of senior probation officers to field staff plus the increased use of an assistant principal probation officer

> To provide adequate assistance for the principal probation officer and to strengthen in particular the administrative structure of supervision in the area.

The circular was welcomed by the National Association of Probation Officers. An editorial in *Probation Journal* stated: 'It should lead to greatly improved opportunities for promotion as well as a more efficient and effective service'.[41]

Between 1966 and 1974 the numbers of assistant chief probation officers in the service increased four-fold.[42] A less dramatic but significant increase in senior probation officers also took place in an effort to reach the suggested 1:5 ratio. The growth of supervisory posts at that time becomes more understandable when we consider the rapid expansion of the service in the 1960s. In 1961, 26 per cent of probation officers in post had less than two years' experience. [43] Bearing in mind that they were engaged in delicate casework counselling as described by King it becomes clear that substantial supervisory resources would be required to ensure 'quality control'.

During these years of rapid expansion the social casework technique remained the main method of intervention used by the probation service. Therefore the somewhat uneasy balance for supervisors, especially senior probation officers, of casework consultant and supervisor was kept. The main reason for the balance surviving appears to have been the ready acceptance for what Haxby describes as 'The advantages to be gained by consultation and casework discussion'. [44] However Haxby goes on:

> The difficult combination of a consultation role with that of an administration in a hierarchy poses problems which are not unique to the probation service. The 2 roles could be accommodated in one person so long as the administrative functions of the service were related almost entirely to how work was organised and did not impinge on the professional responsibility of officers.[45]

However, the professional freedom that many probation officers were trying to retain at that time was already being questioned by developments in the service task. Haxby points out that in 1964 a Home Office circular laid down procedures for the compulsory supervision of young persons released from detention centres. Amongst these was a requirement that officers wishing to discharge a detention centre licence early or apply for recall of a young person would need to have their applications endorsed by their principal probation officer. Haxby quotes Utting:

> Technically the new procedure in requiring endorsement imposed no

22

restrictions on the probation officer but in practice it meant the submission by the probation officer of his opinions to the chief officer for the latter's approval. The probation officer's range of decision making was thus curtailed and his inferior position in the administration hierarchy emphasised.[46]

This was the first of several developments in the service that required officers to get endorsements from their superiors. In 1967 the Criminal Justice Act introduced parole. At the time, the National Association of Probation Officers spoke out stridently against executive decision-making regarding recall procedures in parole cases. They argued that if probation officers felt recall should be considered it should be a matter for the criminal courts. They argued that magistrates should decide if offenders on parole should be recalled as this would ensure that the probation officers' professional authority would be tested by a body outside the service. The National Association of Probation Officers also pointed out that magistrates were in fact service employers, therefore such a procedure could develop magistrates' understanding of the service's task and methods, so enhancing service standing.[47] The Home Office rejected these arguments and reinforced the role of the principal officer.[48] We can see here that both the National Association of Probation Officers and the Home Office had reversed their positions of forty years before. Earlier it had been the Home Office wanting to keep magistrates in touch with the workings of the probation service whilst the National Association of Probation Officers urged moves towards supervisory grades.

By the end of the 1960s the whole process of staff supervision in the probation service was once again being questioned. There were three main lines of query which, when brought together, posed substantial problems regarding supervision in the service. They were:

1   A growing dissatisfaction with casework as a means of working with offenders at all levels in the service.
2   Concern regarding the structure of the service and its ability to facilitate development.
3   Anxiety regarding personal evaluation processes.

Casework in probation had survived a remarkably long time as the main, with some officers the only, technique in working with clients. Training courses had developed with casework skills as the core element in the syllabus. Naturally there was anxiety surrounding any questioning of its effectiveness. Furthermore most people were not feeling that casework did not work, rather that casework was not a relevant approach in many instances. This meant that if as a client you had the right problems and the capacity to be helped via casework the probation service felt it had something to offer. However, the service was increasingly aware that large numbers of offenders had problems that could not be relieved by casework methods, and was widening its thinking on social work issues along with colleagues in other forms of social work and recognising the deficiencies in our intervention techniques. Younghusband stated in 1978:

> Social work had looked at itself before the 1950's but did so more consistently in the energy characteristic of the post war years. Naturally it tried first to learn more about individual and family behaviour. It was dazzled by the key to many inexplicable responses offered by the concepts of unconscious motivation, maternal deprivation, and the mechanics of defence. Only casework existed as a technique.

She develops her point:

> But at national conferences there was regular discussion of social issues, for example bad housing or the iniquities of hire purchase firms. In other words social work techniques were more limited than social work concerns.[49]

Forder in 1966 was more forthright in his criticism of casework in probation:

> The limitations in the contribution of social work to the solution of social problems due to the concentration on social casework in Britain is well illustrated in the field of delinquency. Few people would doubt that group and community pressures play an important part in some forms of delinquency. Yet the main contribution of social work to meeting the problem of delinquency is made by the probation service using casework methods alone.[50]

The desire to have more to offer clients than casework counselling skills put pressure on supervisory grades in three ways:

(a) There was an understandable desire on the part of field staff to turn to their superiors for answers. 'What are our superiors doing in terms of developing professional practice in order that we can help a wider range of clients?'
(b) The innovative flair that the service has been blessed with throughout its history had to be supervised. Suddenly officers wanted to experiment with different forms of groupwork, community work, joint work etc. Many superiors had no knowledge or experience of these new ways of working, therefore what

could they offer in a supervisory capacity? Furthermore, how far should officers be allowed to go before supervisors refused to legitimise their activities?

(c)   Supervisors still needed to ensure their staff developed acceptable casework skills. There was a danger that field staff would confuse the desire to develop new skills to help more clients with the misguided notion that casework was now a completely discredited technique. 'Let's not throw the baby out with the bath water' was a common cry amongst supervisors throughout the seventies.

The second line of thought concerning staff supervision in probation addressed the structure of the service. By the beginning of the 1970s principal officers had not been directly involved with clients for many years. Senior officers had reduced their direct involvement with clients substantially and many felt they also should completely withdraw. The growth of a line management structure had occurred with great speed, vividly demonstrated by Haxby in Tables 2.1 and 2.2.[51]

Table 2.1

Year	A* All grades	B Supervisory	C Non-supervisory	B:C Ratio
1961	1762	241	1521	1:6.31
1964	2167	310	1857	1:5.99
1965	2319	352	1967	1:5.59
1966	2557	439	2118	1:4.82
1967	2745	484	2261	1:4.67
1968	2960	549	2411	1:4.39
1969	3172	590	2582	1:4.38
1970	3352	641	2711	1:4.23
1971	3608	703	2905	1:4.13
1972	3939	807	3132	1:3.88
1973	4327	887	3440	1:3.88
1974	4543	979	3564	1:3.64
1975	4735	1082	3653	1:3.38

*Figures exclude temporary and part-time officers.

Table 2.2

Year	A Senior POs	B Main grade	C Temporary	D B+C	A:D Ratio
1961	158	1521	27	1548	1:9.80
1964	222	1857	17	1874	1:8.44
1968	430	2411	52	2463	1:5.73
1971	565	2905	81	2986	1:5.28
1974	787	3564	129	3693	1:4.69
1975	869	3653	134	3787	1:4.36

The range of tasks the service had in the 1970s had also substantially grown. Probation officers were now working in prisons, the number of hostels was growing fast, parole had arrived and community service was in its infancy, apart from new methods of working with our probationers. Although it could be said that this was an exciting period for the probation service there was an understandable anxiety that we were about to grapple with these exciting new developments with a management structure that had been formed on an assumption that we would be supervising our clients via the traditional casework method. It was in this area that supervisors had their skills which had led to their promotion. The National Association of Probation Officers commented in 1970:

> It is also of great importance to find means to emphasize that the framework of the probation service must always be seen as an 'enabling' structure, rather than a hierarchical organisation in which power concentrates at the top.[52]

The Association was also concerned about the status of the field probation officer:

> There appeared a deep and widespread concern about the growth of structure and its effects upon the individual officer; particularly the erosion of his responsibilities and the lowering of his status, vis à vis the 'higher grades'.[53]

It is unfortunate that during this period much energy seems to have been spent in debating which end of the line management structure was the most important when clearly it was important to improve both areas. Good field officers needed to be recognised and encouraged to develop their skills whilst management needed to develop its skills following a period of rapid growth. To quote Haxby again:

> Emphasising the professional independence of the main grade should not be represented as an alternative to strong management. As the service expands the need for better management becomes apparent. Management is needed for organising work, coordinating effort, controlling the volume of work and keeping checks on its quality, ensuring the facilities and resources to enable the professional task to be satisfactorily discharged and identifying those problems which require a general rather than an individual solution.[54]

There was much talk in the early 1970s of the need to develop a career grade. Whilst there may have been, perhaps still is, a commendable case to make for this grade there was some confusion as to why such a grade seemed desirable. Most of us would probably agree that it makes sense to encourage talented field workers to stay in the field. The structure in the 1970s, as now, entices good field workers to leave the field. Perhaps the most important thing to ensure is that good field workers who remain, because they and their management recognise the contribution they are making at that level, should not suffer financially. In that sense a career grade seems logical. However, it does not follow that the introduction of a career grade would somehow restore autonomy to those workers in that category. Many people in the early part of the decade seemed to be equating a career grade with professional freedom, an equation which seems likely to simply complicate things further. The Butterworth report, although noted in probation circles mainly for its impact on salary scales, did try to address the issue. Butterworth suggested that there should be two grades of field probation officer. 'A' grade would apply to all those joining the service. After three years' experience it would be possible to move to 'B' grade if, following assessment, it was felt sufficient ability had been demonstrated. The 'B' pay scale was significantly better than the 'A' grade scale. Sadly Butterworth's attempt to provide a career grade proved extremely divisive. Firstly there was variation amongst local services in the criteria for moving on to the 'B' grade. Consequently in some areas movement to 'B' grade was virtually a rubber stamp exercise whilst in other areas, refusal to advance officers to the 'B' scale was not uncommon. Secondly in most areas the personal evaluation process which had only just begun was suddenly linked with substantial sums of money and career prospects. Thirdly a procession of divisive appeals began throughout the country leading to a lowering of morale amongst staff, and professional jealousy and intrigue grew like a cancer. It is surprising that Butterworth allowed senior probation officers to be enmeshed in this process as the report had described the role of a senior probation officer as being

> Responsible for the provision of support services, for the allocation of duties, and particularly for the quality of work amongst his team, principally through regular casework supervision and professional advice.[55]

The last area for concern that occupied the thoughts of many in the probation service in the early 1970s was the delicate one of personal evaluations. Of course assessments of staff were not new in that personal references are a form of assessment. However no agreement had been reached on the criteria or procedures for assessment within the service at this point. This is surprising given the size of the service nationally by 1970 but is probably linked to the vexed question of professional freedom. On this basis many probation officers rejected the notion of ongoing assessments by line managers. However until 1968 the Home Office inspectorate had operated a basic assessment process in the form of a confirmation inspection. All officers had to be confirmed in post by the inspectorate and this confirmation could only take place after fairly rigorous scrutiny of case records followed by lengthy case discussions. In 1968 the speed of expansion in the service was such that the inspectorate relinquished this duty although random inspections were still carried out and news that 'the inspectorate were coming' would send teams of officers scurrying off to update their records!

In 1969 a Home Office working party suggested procedures for staff evaluation and how these evaluations might relate to promotion issues. Whilst the National Association of Probation Officers did not disagree with the proposals they did feel that officers should have a right to see the completed evaluation document. Some principal probation officers would not agree to this. This split was unfortunate in that it led to a piecemeal introduction of personal evaluation which was not 'owned' by the National Association of Probation Officers, leading to considerable suspicion about the process at field level. This situation placed the senior probation officer in a difficult position. Seniors were already faced with new interpretations and demands being made of the supervision they should offer. Now they were required to make assessments that would be important documents in terms of their staffs' career prospects. Haxby describes the situation as follows:

> As the inspectorial role of senior staff become more significant there seems to be more possibility of conflict between this function and the work of casework supervisors.

A few lines later he writes: 'If an officer is to make the most of supervisors he must be able to discuss frankly the difficulties he meets'. The point is developed:

> Such disclosures can only be made within a confidential relationship with a professional colleague. It may be difficult for this relationship to develop or for an officer to reveal his problems and weaknesses if the same senior has at another time to prepare a report of his capacities and relate his performance to the possibilities of promotion. Similarly difficulties face the Assistant Chief/Chief Probation Officer who may have to reconcile the need to support and encourage with the duty to inspect and on occasions advise a committee against confirming or promoting an officer or even recommend dismissal.[56]

Haxby broaches the subject of senior casework posts with management responsibilities, and variations of this theme have been tried or considered in other social work agencies. However it has proved difficult, if not impossible so far, to remove the senior probation officer entirely out of the personal evaluation process. The senior is the first line manager in a clearly defined line management system which suggests the answer may lie more in changing the process rather than removing the first manager from the process.

Having moved from the administrative and inspectorial role of the 1930s and 1940s towards the casework consultancy role in the 1950s and 1960s supervisors in the following decade suddenly found that the very technique that they were to be consulted about, namely casework, was in decline and new methods of working were being developed in which they could claim no special expertise. With the very structure of the service also being questioned how were supervisors to react? Perhaps because they were now two steps removed from field work the chief officer role developed in a relatively logical, unproblematic manner. (The title chief officer replaced principal officer after the local government changes in the early 1970s.) Chief Officer grades could clearly be seen in an organisational and development role. There was much to be done in this area and a broad overview was required. The development of policy could be identified as a chief officer task, the effective chief officers realising good policy development could only be achieved if field staff took part in the policy formulation process. There was acceptance of the inspectorial role of chief officer grades particularly as periodic evaluation of individual officers was now accepted throughout the service. The vast majority of the service accepted that staff should be accountable for their actions and that this accountability would normally be to a chief officer. Occasionally issues may have had to be taken by the chief officer to the probation committee, and some officers still argued they were directly accountable to the committee, but these issues and officers with this view were rare.

The development of the senior probation officer role was more difficult. The inspectorial and accountability aspects of the role had always been vague and when difficult issues in this area arose these were often referred to a chief officer, suggesting to field staff that whilst it might have been part of the senior's job to draw attention to poor quality work it was not part of the task to deal with it. However, there was acceptance of the casework advisor role together with local co-ordination of resources and workload management. But these generally accepted roles were now open to question as service practice and structure were scrutinised. Fortunately the probation service were not alone in their difficulties at this stage. With local government reorganisation, social services departments were subjected to great upheaval and social workers were also questioning their practice and reliance on the casework model. Trying to come to terms with this in an article interestingly entitled 'Trial and error' in 1974 Josephine Rowley stated:

> It is crucial that the supervisor is able clearly to define the task that she is expecting the social worker to accomplish. Conversely it is also the responsibility of the senior to ensure that deficiencies in resources and criticism of policy are communicated to the management team.[57]

Rowley is highlighting a crucial issue in this statement. When an organisation is agreed on its task and how to do it (i.e. reduce offending by casework) then line managers are engaged in a predominantly one-way process, this being ensuring staff develop the required skills to undertake the task. However, when agreement on how to undertake the task deteriorates (i.e. casework is not always appropriate) and indeed there may not be agreement as to the task itself, then the line manager is engaged in a two-way process in which communication skills become vital. The senior probation officer in the 1970s needed to learn how to communicate both ways quickly and effectively if policy formulation was to be sound, if resources were to be adequate and effectively used to carry out the priorities agreed within the service.

Focusing on the thorny subject of social work supervision in 1974 Rowley suggested the process should operate at three levels:

1 Regular formal sessions where new work is discussed along with general workload management issues.
2 Response to emergencies. Here Rowley is quick to point out that to offer this facility without the regular formal sessions would be counter-productive serving only to create a high anxiety level.
3 Supervision within the team. There had been in both social services and probation a noticeable movement towards teamwork in the early 1970s. Unfortunately just as with casework twenty years before there was a lot of talking being done without common understanding of the language. This led to claims that 'we are operating a teamwork approach', from seniors who had just discovered the allocation meeting! Nevertheless Rowley suggested supervision within the team should be formalised mainly to avoid haphazard approaches to the task and the danger of wrong information being passed on.

It was the development of social work practice and its implications for probation that pointed the way forward for senior probation officers in the 1970s. As officers developed groupwork skills, became more involved in shared working and adopted a higher profile in the community it became necessary for them to communicate with each other much more. No longer could a group of officers operate as individuals, counselling on a one to one basis in their separate offices meeting only at coffee time to swop 'treatment plans'. They needed to share their work, knowledge, skills and interests as a team and from this movement emerged the model of senior probation officer as team leader.

What is teamwork? Perhaps the sensible approach to this issue would be to allow teams to develop their own model of teamwork as probation teams around the country have vastly different problems to tackle with widely differing resources available to them. As with all things the teamwork approach has evolved since it began to gain ground in the early 1970s. David Millard wrote in 1978:

> Teamwork starts with the notion that instead of regarding each officer as an individual with prescribed statutory duties, it makes more sense to think of the work group as a team possessing a pool of resources to be differentially deployed.

In this way Millard suggested that 'The probation office can become much more than a casework agency'.[58]

Whilst it may appear that teamwork sprang naturally from developing probation practice this is not to say that it was accepted with ease by officers or seniors. Officers of many years experience were not used to sharing in this manner and many found the approach threatening coming as it did at a time when their traditional skills were being questioned and they were being asked to undertake new tasks in a new way. Some seniors found themselves being pressed by their staff to move towards a teamwork approach when they had very little experience of working with groups in this way and were concerned about its implications. Some seniors felt that teamwork amounted to an abdication of responsibility by senior probation officers.

Even if a senior and his staff wanted to adopt this approach it would mean many hours of meetings in which the objectives, structure, policies and methods of the team would be discussed. These negotiations could take months and during the meetings senior and staff would be learning how to relate to each other in different ways. There was need for trust in the group in order that strengths and weaknesses could be explored, and an overall philosophy on which the team could agree would ideally emerge. My own experience is that unless this intangible quality emerges from the team's deliberations — a vision of what could be if everything in and around the team worked perfectly — then in the long term the teamwork approach will collapse. It is a time consuming threatening process which needs a vision to sustain it when there are setbacks, and there will be plenty of those!

During this period the senior may well find he/she is called upon to display considerable groupwork expertise and it is perhaps not a coincidence that the teamwork approach began to gain ground a few years after the service started to develop its groupwork skills. Peter Lewis referring to his experience as a senior trying to develop a teamwork approach suggests seniors require 'The skills of a group-worker to facilitate communication, to help the group handle its disappointments and frustrations and work at the inevitable conflicts'.[59] Lewis describes in detail his approach to teamwork and the process he and his team went through. He comments: 'It has been wisely suggested that the senior learns his role from his team'. Furthermore he suggests that 'The senior has to negotiate his contract'.[60]

Having been through the process of moving into a teamwork approach the senior may well find he has a role quite unlike the traditional role of a senior probation officer. Certainly this would have been the case in the 1970s. This role would need to be legitimised by management. Lewis suggested that apart from the delicate skills required to keep the group together in a well-motivated form, the senior should also identify pressure points, establish priorities and bid for resources. Lastly Lewis suggested that 'It means looking at one's own work and evaluating its effectiveness'.[61]

Whilst the movement towards teamwork may have made sense in the 1970s, as a way of developing service practice, what were the implications for the supervision of staff? It is perhaps interesting to note that many officers who do not like to be controlled by supervisors seem quite happy to be controlled by their peer group if they have a say in the process. Ieuan Miles noted recently: 'Effective teamwork depends very much on collaborative work which by definition curtails individual autonomy'.[62]

Anybody looking at teamwork in the 1970s can see examples of this. Officers who would have objected strongly if their superiors had asked to see a court report recommending custody for further consideration before it appeared in court, seemed quite happy to bring these reports to teams for further discussion. A close look at a well-thought-out teamwork approach within a probation setting will reveal that the staff involved have to exercise considerable self-discipline, surrender a degree of professional autonomy, and accept considerable responsibility for ensuring good standards of practice are adhered to and good support systems for individuals are available. Returning to Lewis again:

> Not the least of its advantages (teamwork) was in giving each officer a stronger support system, formalizing and strengthening the value of consultations amongst colleagues.[63]

Whilst the introduction of teamwork may have been helpful in developing professional practice and support systems what did it mean in terms of accountability and the inspectorial role of supervisors? Clearly management could not abdicate responsibility for these issues. In the early days of teamwork development perhaps the boundaries of accountability were not always as well defined as they might have been and assistant chief probation officers are probably more aware now of the need to ratify teamwork arrangements and agree on areas of accountability. Teams are normally quite happy to be held accountable for what goes on within the team. However, there must be a point at which the senior probation officer is held accountable to an assistant chief probation officer regarding team activity. Thus the senior's role may have changed but the responsibility has not. This situation highlights the need for assistant chief probation officers and seniors to develop their supervisory relationship. The inspectorial role of chief officer grades is not sufficient in this situation as the senior will want to know if the team and its work is 'owned' by management. This is vital as it will affect management's attitude to resourcing the team and provide support for the senior and the team as it further develops its practice. The line management process should not feel threatened by teamwork. It is still necessary. However, line managers need to share the responsibility for improving practice rather than develop policy and then review how closely it is being carried out in an inspectorial role a few months later. Millard raised this issue:

> The 'line management' model of accountability is clearly appropriate for a situation in which people at the front line are operating as individuals and all of them are doing the same task. But if only one or 2 of them are doing that and the rest of them are differentially employed on anything from constructive groupwork to setting up housing associations and running volunteer groups, and if moreover over a period of time they are juggling these roles between them, in those circumstances the relevance of line management becomes problematical.[64]

Millard went on to suggest that the old style local case committee could be restored to which the senior probation officer could be accountable. Chief officers could then be accountable to the main probation committee and could inspect and advise teams but not control them. This, according to Millard, would free chief officer grades for more developmental work. This is almost the opposite to the sharing role described earlier. Millard seems to place the chief officer grade in a consultancy role with teams. However, both suggestions highlight the need for management to review staff supervision when a teamwork approach is operating. Teamwork suggests a break from the straightforward line management at the lower levels. This has implications for chief officer grades. Millard describes the problem as being essentially a shift of emphasis from a line management inspectorial role for chief officers to a more innovative role, suggesting that at present the inspectorial role forces chief officers to see innovation as a luxury. He does not suggest unfettered autonomy for teams, rather more opportunity for chief officers to share in their development.

It is perhaps surprising to find that with the development of teamwork the difficult area of personal evaluation, much talked about in the early 1970s, was not incorporated into the teamwork process. There have been experiments in team evaluation of individuals, in some cases teams have evaluated the seniors' performances and this has been incorporated into the formal management evaluation process, but these developments have never been more than isolated examples. Maybe it was considered wise not to bring such a potentially explosive issue into teams that were only beginning to work together as a group resource to clients. However, it could be argued that there is little point in developing trust, openness, etc. within a group if it is not used to cope with the most difficult problems. My own experience of the team evaluation process is that whilst it can be a very helpful experience it does need the backing of all team members. As it is quite likely that in any group of probation staff there is at least one person who either disagrees with the process in principle or is unwilling to co-operate due to a previously poor experience, this may account for the rare examples of team evaluation.

This situation left the senior probation officer of the 1970s in an uncomfortable position — trying to encourage staff to work closely together and develop new ways of working whilst at the same time being a gatekeeper to promotional opportunities via the evaluation process. There is no doubt that the evaluation document is a powerful document in terms of career prospects even if it does not always achieve its original objectives of being the basis for on-going supervision. This situation is problematic enough but when one considers the vagaries surrounding the evaluation process one can only admire those seniors who manage to keep a healthy atmosphere in their teams. Rowley describes just a few of the problems.

1 Setting standards of performance. How is this to be done?
2 What is normal or average?
3 How can subjective judgement be minimised?
4 Should the stage of a person's career be relevant?
5 What level of anxiety is provoked by the process itself?[65]

Other issues include:

(a) What is their purpose?
(b) How reliable is the assessment?
(c) What should be evaluated? (Records? Reports? Court performance? Community work? Sit in on interviews? Consult clients?)
(d) How should this be done and who should be involved? (Should magistrates or clients or community links be contacted?)

Whatever the procedure adopted the person evaluated can claim it is deficient if he does not like the end result. Since the 1970s there have been numerous examples of staff who feel they have been unfairly treated in evaluations and feel the matter has not been satisfactorily resolved, or the criticism proved or justified. This has become almost a way of life for the supervisory grades, the response being that the procedure may not be very good but we must have something, and it's all we have.

At least during the 1970s, despite the increasingly complex nature of professional issues surrounding staff supervision, the confusion as to whether the service was supervised by magistrates or professional supervisors was largely resolved. Whilst probation committees would still expect to deal with serious disciplinary matters the day to day supervision of probation officers is now clearly with the supervisory grades. The 1972 Criminal Justice Act relieved case committees of the duty to review individual cases and replaced the case committee with the liaison committee who were expected to share issues related to the courts and the probation service in a more generalised form. This finally clarified the dilemma that Phylidda Parsloe illustrated:

> This double structure of seniors and principal probation officers and committee of magistrates each with some overlapping functions has made it difficult for the service to be clear as to the role of its senior officers.[66]

The 1972 Act virtually ended the argument that probation officers were accountable to the court for their work.

It would be wrong to suggest that by the 1980s all senior probation officers were operating a teamwork approach. Such developments were still quite rare and often resisted by officers and supervisory grades alike. There are still groups of officers in the country who receive supervision on a one to one basis and who receive their allocation of work with little or no discussion. This may not be inappropriate. Much will depend on the area the team is operating in, its resources and the manner in which it goes about its tasks. However, as we moved into the 1980s the senior probation officer role was on the move again! For the first time seniors were being called managers. The traditional induction courses for new senior probation officers in the Midlands region became a new managers' course. We began to hear the role described as a resource manager, the implication being that the senior would be the co-ordinator of a range of resources with the objective of maximising their efficiency.

The 1980s began in disappointing fashion for the probation service. The long awaited Management Structure Review[67] was published in 1980 but was seen by many as a non event, an opportunity missed. It suggested little change and even resurrected the senior practitioner idea, only a few years after the conflict stemming from Butterworth's 'A' and 'B' grades. In a critical response Jenny Kirkpatrick, general secretary of the National Association of Probation Officers at that time, described the confusion in the report as to the meaning of 'management', what its purpose was and what its style should be.

> Never raised in the report are the questions to be raised for all but most senior managers. 'What is your job': Is it to manage on behalf of employers, or is it to coordinate and enable on behalf of colleague officers.[68]

This was just one of many criticisms of a rather bland report. Meanwhile there were signs that chief officer grades were moving towards the developmental role that Millard suggested. However, this did not lead to team leaders along the lines that Millard felt appropriate, a new role as policy implementors and monitors began to emerge. For example, Greater Manchester Probation Service management produced a document entitled, 'Priority areas of work in the Probation Service'.[69] This led to considerable debate in that area concerning who makes policy, why and how. An article in the *Probation Journal* at that time described the paper as 'A long term strategy for the service, non-negotiable but open to comment and discussion'. Later the article describes, 'The development of a programme of monitoring to ensure priorities were kept to and to help to determine the allocation of resources'.[70]

It was claimed that this far-reaching policy document was drawn up in consultation only with chief officer grades although the service management insisted they had borne the views of staff and the National Association of Probation Officers in mind. However the chief probation officer of Manchester did not attempt to hide his view that chief officer grades were there to develop policy. He strongly defended the view that 'There is a need for senior members of the probation service to take the initiative and to give a clear lead'.[71] This development of roles between chief officer grades and senior probation officers was given further impetus by the Home Office statement of objectives and priorities in 1984. The Home Office provided for the first time a broad view of their intentions for the service nationally in the short and medium term. Service managements were left in no doubt as to the priorities the Home Office wished to see resources being centred upon. Service managements were left to develop their own local statements of objectives and priorities based on the national statement.

Although many services engaged in extensive consultations with staff before producing their local statements this task clearly pushed chief officer grades more exclusively into the role of policy makers. Furthermore it was obvious that the movement towards these objectives and priorities would need to be regularly reviewed and the pivot of these reviews was likely to be the senior probation officer grades. They would be responsible for moving teams towards the stated goals and reporting back on progress. They would be held accountable for their progress towards the stated goals by chief officers. Thus seniors have a policy monitoring role whilst officers themselves become policy implementors. This looks to be a somewhat oppressive framework for field officers and if the process is to succeed it seems likely that much will depend on the communication skills of supervisors. To quote Ieuan Miles:

> The only effective course open to management in reconciling concerns about loss of autonomy with the need to pursue organisational goals is to demonstrate that there is a congruence between the aspirations of the organisation and the professional aims and objectives of the individual practitioner. . . . The professional practitioner must be given the opportunity to influence the organisation by drawing upon the vital intelligence he possesses about clients, courts and the community at large. To enable officers to do this effectively managers need to be very conscious of encouraging the flow of communication and their style of management.[72]

The emerging role for seniors in terms of how they supervise their staff seems to be much less vague and seniors have been complaining about the vagueness of their role for years. It would seem that in the next few years targets will be more clearly laid down and priority tasks identified. Seniors will have resources in terms of staff and financial budgets. Their task will be to move as close as possible to the targets and inform management about developments and problems involved. Staff supervision is likely therefore to be more closely focused on the teams' targets and how each individual is contributing towards those. This sounds rather mechanistic and if seniors appear mechanistic in their approach they are likely to be in difficulty with their staff. Officers will need to feel there is sufficient flexibility to allow teams to respond to the needs of their clients in ways that do not always conform at first sight to the current statement of local objectives and priorities. This seems essential if new ideas are to be tried and innovation encouraged. Perhaps the supervisory role in this situation is not to respond by saying 'We can't do this, it does not conform to the Statement of Local Objectives and Priorities', rather 'If we do this we must evaluate the project including how it relates to the Statement of Local Objectives and Priorities'.

The senior probation officer role of resource manager and policy monitor may well become a more clearly defined role than the officer's role of previous decades. However, many of the earlier problems are still present. The senior must still encourage, support and motivate. The evaluation process remains. Accountability cannot and must not go away. Thus as the role emerges it may well be that the skills of a group leader will be highlighted. Communications up and down the line management system will be vital if the refining of local statements of objectives and priorities is to be a genuine improvement. Helping individuals towards a constructive role in the team will be vital as will be an awareness of the group's responsibilities to its clients and its employers. Raynor, commenting on the National Statement of Objectives and Priorities, writes:

> Managerial supervision would need to be widened to include evaluative skills, community skills, an understanding of criminal justice systems as a target for incremental change and a fuller awareness of collective responsibility beyond the individual workload of individual officers.[73]

The 1980s have also seen another possibility emerge regarding staff supervision — the seniorless team. For approximately a quarter of a century we have retained the notion that there should be supervisors on a ratio of 1:5. Thus teams usually consist of five or six officers with one or two assistants. Assistant chiefs normally supervise five or six seniors. Much above that and chief officers begin to think of an extra assistant chief. This ratio does not of course exist solely because of supervisory duties but supervision is often given as a primary reason. But is this ratio correct? Practice has changed, support systems are changing, roles within the service have changed. Could resources be redistributed more efficiently?

It was hoped that the ill-fated management structure review would produce some indicators on these issues but little emerged. However, there has been an interesting experiment in Nottinghamshire. A team of officers working with homelessness have been operating without a senior, at least in the conventional sense. An article by Green and Glanfield in 1983 suggests that whilst there may have been organisational problems it has been a most rewarding exercise in terms of staff supervision. The staff refer to themselves as the 'client servicing group' and the senior probation officer role within the group is shared on a rota basis. Staff supervision is described as being on a weekly basis, every fourth week being a group exercise. The other three weeks allow two individuals to be supervised in small groups. Personal evaluations involve the whole group with the senior probation officer and assistant chief probation officer brought in at a later stage to endorse the process. Green and Glanfield talk of the need for all members of the team to be conscientious and disciplined but that the end result is very positive. They describe their experience as follows: 'Group supervision feels remarkably honest and helpful. It occurs in a regular and planned way.' They go on to say that 'It seems that a structure that offers its members a more real participation in decision making works better and is more satisfying'. Finally they write:

> It may be that while we are seen to deliver an efficient, useful and caring service to our defined client group then our system is endorsed. Perhaps this kind of accountability is appropriate and such a measurement should not be resisted but endorsed.[74]

As we move through the 1980s it may well be that the service continues to develop at the remarkably rapid pace of the last sixty years. Supervisors must continue to adapt their supervisory skills to the needs of the service and those who work in it. However the core issues are likely to remain the same. We are a caring service and those with the supervisory role wish to care for their staff. However accountability issues must be squarely faced up to. This is very difficult when you have two masters. In a sense this has always been so. There are our employers and there are our clients. As professional 'carers' clients must come first. As employees we are ultimately accountable to our employers. Jenny Roberts focused on this dilemma in 1984 when addressing the National Association of Probation Officers professional conference.

> We cannot, I think, assume the perspectives and concerns of managers and practitioners are united and identical. We are exposed to different levels of demand from different clients and we have different primary accountabilities.

Making her point with dramatic clarity she went on:

> In some senses the interests of our respective primary client groups are diametrically opposed — for it is my committee which sentences your clients.[75]

Notes

1   Bochel, Dorothy, *Probation and After Care Service*, Scottish Academic Press, 1976.
2   Ibid.
3   King, Joan, *The Probation and After Care Service*, Butterworths, 1969.
4   Bochel, Dorothy, *Probation and After Care Service*, Scottish Academic Press, 1976.
5   Leeson, Cecil, *The Probation System*, P.S. King & Son, London, 1914.
6   HOC, 1914.
7   Baird Committee Report, 1920.
8   Ibid.
9   1925 Criminal Justice Bill.
10 1926 Probation Rules.
11 Bochel, Dorothy, *Probation and After Care Service*, Scottish Academic Press, 1976.
12 King, Joan, *The Probation and After Care Service*, Butterworths, 1969.
13 Review of social work in courts, 1935.
14 Ibid.
15 Bochel, Dorothy, *Probation and After Care Service*, Scottish Academic Press, 1976.
16 Review of social work in courts, 1935.
17 Ibid.
18 Ibid.
19 Bochel, Dorothy, *Probation and After Care Service*, Scottish Academic Press, 1976.

20 Ibid.
21 Probation Rules 1949.
22 Jarvis, F., *Advise, Assist and Befriend — A History of the Probation and After Care Service*, Butterworths, 1972.
23 Haxby, David, *Probation*, Constable, 1978.
24 The Morison Report, 1962.
25 Byrne, P.S., *Learning to Care, Person to Person*, Churchill, Livingstone, 1973.
26 Ibid.
27 King, Joan, *The Probation Service*, NAPO, 1958.
28 Kadushin, A., *Consultation in Social Work*, Columbia University Press, 1977.
29 Gorman, Joanne, *Some Characteristics of Consultation*, National Association of Social Workers, New York, 1963.
30 Byrne, P.S., *Learning to Care, Person to Person*, Churchill, Livingstone, 1973.
31 Mattinson, Janet, *The Reflective Process in Casework Supervision*, Institute of Marital Studies, 1975.
32 Kadushin, A., *Consultations in Social Work*, Columbia University Press, 1977.
33 Report of Departmental Committee on the Probation Service, Chairman Mr R.P. Morison QC, HMSO Cmnd 1650, 1962.
34 Kadushin, A., *Consultations in Social Work*, Columbia University Press, 1977.
35 Monger, M., *Casework in Probation*, Butterworths, 1972.
36 Ibid.
37 Probation Papers, *Seniority in the Probation Service*, NAPO, 1966.
38 King, Joan, *The Probation and After Care Service*, Butterworths, 1969.
39 Etzioni, A. (ed.), *The Semi Professionals and their Organisations*.
40 HOC (see Haxby).
41 Haxby, David, *Probation*, Constable, 1978.
42 Ibid.
43 Ibid.
44 Ibid.
45 Ibid.
46 Ibid.
47 Ibid.
48 Ibid.
49 Younghusband, E., *Social Work in Britain 1950-75, Volume 1*, George Allen and Unwin, 1978.
50 Forder, A., *Social Casework and Administrator*, 1966.

51   Haxby, David, *Probation*, Constable, 1978.
52   NAPO Working Party on the Structure of the Probation Service Report, *Probation Journal*, 1970.
53   Ibid.
54   Haxby, David, *Probation*, Constable, 1978.
55   Report of the Butterworth Inquiry, HMSO, Cmnd 5076, 1972.
56   Haxby, David, *Probation*, Constable, 1978.
57   Rowley, J., 'Trial and error', *Social Work Today*, vol. 5, no. 14, 1974.
58   Millard, D., 'Teamwork in probation. Prospects and implications', *Social Work Today*, vol. 9, no. 36, 1978.
59   Lewis, P., 'An approach to teamwork', *Social Work Today*, vol. 9, no. 36, 1978.
60   Ibid.
61   Ibid.
62   Miles, I., 'Professionalism and social work' (unpublished), 1985.
63   Lewis, P., 'An approach to teamwork', *Social Work Today*, vol. 9, no. 36, 1978.
64   Millard, D., 'Teamwork in probation. Prospects and implications', *Social Work Today*, vol. 9, no. 36, 1978.
65   Rowley, J., 'Trial and error', *Social Work Today*, vol. 5, no. 14, 1974.
66   Parsloe, Phylidda, *The Work of the Probation and After-Care Officer*, Routledge and Kegan Paul, 1967.
67   Report of the Working Party on Management Structure in the Probation Service, 1980.
68   Kirkpatrick, J., 'The management structure review. A response', *Probation Journal*, vol. 27, no. 4, 1980.
69   Greater Manchester Probation Service, *Priority Areas of Work in the Probation Service*, 1980.
70   Adams, S., Moss, L. and Pleasance, G., 'Who makes policy: How and why?', *Probation Journal*, vol. 27, no. 4, 1980.
71   Marsh, J.W., 'A response to who makes policy: How and why?', *Probation Journal*, vol. 27, no. 4, 1980.
72   Miles, I., 'Professionalism and social work' (unpublished), 1985.
73   Raynor, P., 'National objectives and priorities: A comment', *Probation Journal*, vol. 31, no. 2, 1984.
74   Green, J. and Glanfield, P., '"Seniorless" teamwork with homeless clients', *Probation Journal*, vol. 30, no. 4, 1983.
75   Roberts, J., *Management, Innovation and Probation Practice*, NAPO, 1984.

3 Research design and instruments

Establishing current practice regarding the supervisory process, analysing its effectiveness and exploring possibilities for the future required the gathering of a great deal of variable data. Information was needed concerning both the quantity and quality of the current supervisory process. Furthermore the views of both the receivers and givers of supervision were vital.

The staff supervision historical review outlined in the previous chapter has tried to integrate key aspects of the subject whilst highlighting crucial developments in chronological order. This review proved very helpful to the author in refining the objectives of the research. Knowledge of the history of staff supervision in our service, an understanding of how supervision objectives have ebbed and flowed, how supervisors and supervisees have perceived changes in practice, is vital if we are to understand what is happening now and look to the future. Many of the comments heard whilst researching the topic have their roots embedded in service history.

Having reviewed the objectives of the research it was clear that a great deal of factual information regarding the current state of practice was needed. Basic questions such as 'are we all receiving formal supervision?' had to be asked. Quantitative research methods seemed most appropriate for obtaining this information, in this case using questionnaires. It was also important that feelings and opinions as to the nature of staff supervision were sought. To a certain extent a well-designed questionnaire could obtain data concerning feelings, perceptions and opinions, but the very nature of questionnaires would encourage a brevity that could over simplify issues. Therefore a qualitative element was built into the research design by way of personal interviews with 10 per cent of those receiving questionnaires. The interviews were carried out after the questionnaires had been returned and scrutinised. An *aide memoire*, based on comments regularly made on returned questionnaires, was drawn up to assist the interviewer. The intention was to amplify issues raised by the questionnaire responses whilst also offering an opportunity for those interviewed to express their feelings about staff supervision more fully than questionnaires would allow.

The views of three grades of staff were obtained: probation officer, senior probation officer and assistant chief probation officer. Whilst the views from these grades concerned the same basic issues, the different grades would obviously be looking at the issues from different perspectives. It was therefore not possible to send all three grades the same questionnaire. Separate questionnaires were designed for each grade, addressing the same issues but acknowledging the different roles within the service each grade has.

Knowing that staff in the service are invariably pressed for time it was necessary to design a questionnaire that would be simple to complete and not take more than fifteen to thirty minutes. Therefore, where possible, answers required no more than a tick in a box. It was also clear from preliminary investigations that when talking about staff supervision, comments about the extent of 'informal supervision' would be made. Therefore the questionnaire made it clear that it was addressing 'formal pre-arranged supervision' and responses should be related to this type of supervision. The question of informal supervision could be looked at during interviews at a later stage. Opportunities were provided within the questionnaires to amplify or add to responses if respondents so wished.

It was clearly necessary to test out these questionnaires by way of a pilot study. As the intention was to use the ten counties within the Midlands region for the main project, a large service outside this area was felt to be an appropriate test bed. It was not difficult to find such a service willing to take part but it did take two months to complete the pilot study. There is no criticism of the service involved here, it is simply a fact of life that permission at various levels has to be obtained and this can take several weeks. The pilot was sent to twenty probation officers, ten senior probation officers and four assistant chief probation officers. Each questionnaire was sent out with a note attached requesting feedback on its design. Respondents were most helpful in this respect, and also provided many comments regarding how they felt about answering the questions and in many cases the questions themselves. This enabled a number of improvements to be made to the questionnaires (Appendix 1).

Further analysis of the pilot responses suggested thought be given to the possibility of having the full project analysed by computer. Clearly this would save a lot of time and provide a great deal more detailed and accurate information than could be obtained by manual analysis. However, much depended on the cost that would be incurred and the designing of a suitable program. Following protracted negotiations and substantial professional assistance, this possibility eventually became reality. However, to transfer the data to computer required further refinements to the questionnaires (Appendix 2).

Whilst the questionnaires were being amended for the last time, the Association of Chief Officers of Probation (ACOP) had been expressing concern regarding the amount of research the service was being asked to take part in, some of it apparently of little relevance to service development. They decided that before chief officers agree to further projects ACOP should have given their approval. At one stage this seemed problematical as ACOP at national level would not be able to give permission for several weeks. Fortunately as the research was to be undertaken only in the Midlands region, it only required the Midlands region of ACOP to approve and this they did very speedily. However it was still necessary to obtain permission from each individual chief probation officer to approach staff and this required a further four weeks. The responsibility for the delays in obtaining permission to carry out the research clearly lies with the author who should have realised that chief officers need time to consult properly with appropriate staff before giving approval. Whilst all chief officers did give permission for staff to be approached this did not in any way restrict the right of any individual approached during the survey to decline to take part.

The questionnaires were eventually sent out in February 1986, within days of the 1986 probation directory being published. This was extremely helpful as using the most up-to-date directory meant that new entrants to the service were included. Clearly first-year officers are of particular concern when considering the supervision of staff. A further advantage was that few people had changed office since the directory was published, therefore few questionnaires were 'lost' due to change of base.

One hundred probation officers, fifty senior probation officers and twenty assistant chief probation officers were selected from the directory using random sampling tables. Each received a questionnaire with an accompanying letter explaining the objectives of the research and guaranteeing anonymity of both service and individuals (Appendix 3). Three weeks later a further letter was sent out thanking those who had responded and gently reminding those who had not (Appendix 4).

Two weeks later the questionnaires so far returned were manually analysed, particularly the additional comments made by respondents. From these comments a number of themes emerged and these formed the basis of the *aide memoire* the researcher used for subsequent interviews (Appendix 5). At this point 10 per cent of those originally sent questionnaires were selected, once again at random, for interviews. There could have been a problem at this point as those selected for interview could have already declined to be involved and not returned their questionnaire. However, nobody contacted did decline to be interviewed, therefore interviews took place in various counties during April 1986.

On average the interviews took 1½ hours, although some were substantially longer. In some interviews not all items on the *aide memoire* were covered. Sometimes this was due to items not being applicable, in others interviewees were wanting to express thoughts and feelings about staff supervision that were not on the *aide memoire*. This was allowed as the researcher felt it important to allow interviewees as free a hand as possible to express views.

Having designed the interview *aide memoire* it was possible to refer the completed questionnaires to the computer operators for analysis. This occurred in early April 1986 and print-outs were available for assessment in May. A few questionnaires arrived after the main bulk had been sent to the computer department. These were subsequently checked with computer print-outs and rarely affected the results. Where there is a noticeable difference it has been mentioned.

One section of the research findings concerns itself with specialists in the probation service. Discussions with specialists suggested they had a number of specific problems related to the nature of the service, its management and its communication systems. Therefore, a separate, small piece of research was undertaken regarding the position of specialists. Ten probation officers were asked to complete Likert's questionnaire on styles of management (Appendix 6). On their return sixteen members of staff operating in a specialist capacity were interviewed using an *aide memoire* (Appendix 7). The information from the *aide memoires* was then tabulated and formed the basis of findings written up in that section.

The last stage of the process — analysing the computer print-outs and making links with the notes taken of interviews — was a lengthy one.

4 Research findings

Introduction

A total of 170 questionnaires was sent out, 153 (90 per cent) were returned. The percentage of returns finally worked out as follows:

Table 4.1

	Returned questionnaires	
	Number	%
Assistant chief officers	20	100
Senior probation officers	44	88
Probation officers	89	89

Unfortunately a few of the returned questionnaires came in too late for computer analysis. Therefore the computer analysis is based on a response rate as follows:

Table 4.2

	Returned questionnaires	
	Number	%
Assistant chief officers	18	90
Senior probation officers	42	84
Probation officers	86	86

However, the comments made by those late respondents have been included in the analysis. Nobody refused to take part in subsequent interviews.

The findings have been divided into sections which are mainly based on the questionnaire plus issues stemming from questionnaires that were looked into at the interview stage.

Frequency of supervision

There seems to be a lot of myths and fantasies within the service concerning the amount of time we should be putting into supervision. It is also particularly difficult to measure if the notion of informal supervision is an acceptable one to the service. The majority of respondents feel that informal supervision is an important supplement to the formal supervision that has been agreed. However, in some cases it seems to be virtually all that is on offer and, based on this research, this approach does not seem acceptable to any grade.

Many respondents commented on the apparent increase in the amount of supervisory activity within the service. To quote an assistant chief probation officer 'supervision is more rigorous — there's more of it'. This officer put forward an interesting reason for the increase. Commenting on service developments in recent years he stated 'the Senior Probation officer validates in the absence of empirical evidence'. But is there 'more of it?'. A senior probation officer commenting on his experience and observations of supervision stated with some feeling 'Some say they do it and don't. There's a lot of covering up.'

Before considering how much supervision is provided it seems reasonable to first ascertain if formal pre-arranged supervision was generally on offer at all. Analysis of returned questionnaires provides the following information:

1 83.3 per cent of chief officer grades say they receive formal pre-arranged supervision.
2 92.9 per cent of senior probation officers say they receive formal pre-arranged supervision.
3 81.4 per cent of probation officers say they receive formal pre-arranged supervision.

These figures are broadly in agreement with the answers given by the main providers of supervision, i.e. line managers: 85.7 per cent of seniors and 100 per cent of assistant chiefs say they provide formal pre-arranged supervision.

However the 85.7 per cent figure attributed to senior probation officers becomes more substantial if it is borne in mind that the samples were randomly selected. Thus 4 per cent of the senior probation officers did not have staff to supervise. A further 4 per cent made comments that suggested the reasons were of a positive nature stemming from a review of supervision systems. Therefore assistant chiefs and seniors have stated clearly that almost without fail they are providing formal pre-arranged supervision where it is appropriate. However 18.6 per cent of field staff claim they are not receiving formal supervision. Reasons given for this state of affairs varied, including:

'Secondment to a day centre, I take part in group supervision but this does not include looking at my work.'
'Secondment to a multi-agency (team) – supervision by team.'
'The system fell into disuse about seven years ago.'
'We tend to discuss things as and when they arise.'
'Senior probation officer ill – no formal supervision for twelve months.'
'Informal supervision via colleagues.'
'My senior attaches little importance to it.'
'Senior probation officer either does not have time or gives it no priority.'
'Senior not interested.'
'In my confirmation year there was little, then it dwindled to none.'

There could have been some confusion as to the exact meaning of the term 'formal pre-arranged supervision', which could account for some of the discrepancy. However, this figure is similar to that found by NAPO in the East Midlands via a survey in 1984. Perhaps there is some truth in the suggestion that there is 'covering up'.

Having established that 81.4 per cent of probation officers do receive formal supervision Table 4.3 gives a breakdown of the frequency of supervision.

Table 4.3 Approximately how often do you receive supervision?

	Absolute frequency	Percentage	Cumulative percentage
Never	16	18.6	18.6
Annually	1	1.2	19.8
½ yearly	2	2.3	22.1
Quarterly	3	3.5	25.6
Bi-monthly	8	9.3	34.9
Monthly	48	55.8	90.7
Fortnightly	6	7.0	97.7
Weekly	2	2.3	100.0

We can see clearly that most officers receive supervision on a monthly basis. However, many people may be concerned that 34.9 per cent of probation officers appear to be receiving formal supervision bi-monthly at best.

In the random sample of field staff there were only two first year officers, one receiving supervision weekly and one monthly. Clearly no statistical significance could be attached to such a small number. However, much concern is expressed regarding the supervision of new staff and it was possible (Table 4.4) to bring out the responses of seniors to their first-year staff, not only officers but first-year assistants.

Table 4.4   How often do you provide formal supervision?

	First-year assistants (%)	First-year officers (%)
Not applicable	45.1	23.8
Quarterly	3.2	0
Monthly	6.5	0
3 Weekly	3.2	0
Fortnightly	22.6	14.3
10 Days	3.2	11.9
Weekly	16.1	50.0

We can see clearly that senior probation officers based on their own returns felt that supervising first year officers requires a much more intensive approach than for new assistants. Given the developing and crucial role often played by probation assistants in the 1980s it may be that further thought should be given to the needs of new probation assistants.

With regard to the supervision of senior probation officers the presence of formal supervision is generally accepted. Chief officer grades were unanimous that they provide it and 92.9 per cent of seniors acknowledged they were receiving it. However there was disagreement regarding the frequency of supervision as Table 4.5, which relates to supervision of first year senior probation officers, illustrates.

Table 4.5 suggests strongly that there is a substantial gap between the supervision assistant chiefs feel they are providing and the supervision seniors feel they are receiving. Once again there could have been some difference of opinion regarding the definition of 'formal pre-arranged supervision' but it is unlikely to account for such contrasting figures. The numbers of first-year senior probation officers in the samples were fairly small. (The senior probation officer sample contained thirteen in their first year. The assistant chief probation officer sample contained eighteen senior probation officers in their first year. These would not necessarily be the same senior probation officers.) Some allowance must be made for that, but

Table 4.5   How often do first year senior probation
officers receive formal supervision?

	SPO response (%)	ACPO response (%)
Not applicable	0	11.1
Never	15.2	0
½ Yearly	7.6	0
Quarterly	0	0
Bi-monthly	15.2	0
Monthly	62.0	16.5
3 Weekly	0	5.6
Fortnightly	0	44.5
10 Days	0	11.1
Weekly	0	5.6
No response	0	5.6

nevertheless there may well be a case for reviewing the quantity of
supervision first-year seniors receive. The two grades generally agreed
on the quantity of supervision provided for experienced seniors,
standard practice appearing to be monthly meetings.

Table 4.6   How often do experienced seniors
receive formal supervision?

	SPO response (%)	ACPO response (%)
Never	9.2	0
½ Yearly	2.3	0
Quarterly	2.3	0
Bi-monthly	11.5	0
6 Weekly	2.3	0
Monthly	72.4	88.9
Fortnightly	0	5.6
No response	0	5.6

A familiar comment made in probation offices around the country
runs something like 'Chief officers are out of touch with what is going
on at grass roots level'. The manner in which chief officers responded
to this research suggests that certainly so far as supervising staff is
concerned this may be something of a myth. Tables 4.7–4.10
demonstrate that chief officers are quite often involved in some depth
in the supervision of field staff.

Many people may be surprised reading Tables 4.7–4.10 that
assistant chiefs are sometimes involved in weekly supervisory sessions
with field staff including in one case a probation assistant. Reading
the additional comments made on questionnaires by chief officers
most of this involvement is likely to be linked to a special responsibility such as a hostel, or a particular service initiative. In some
cases with first-year staff, there may be some doubts concerning

51

Table 4.7 How often do assistant chiefs supervise first-year officers?

	Absolute frequency	Percentage
Not applicable	8	44.4
Annually	1	5.6
Quarterly	1	5.6
Weekly	3	16.7
No response	5	27.8

Table 4.8 How often do chief officers supervise officers with more than three years' experience?

	Absolute frequency	Percentage
Not applicable	7	38.9
Annually	2	11.1
Monthly	4	22.2
No response	5	27.8

Table 4.9 How often do assistant chiefs supervise first-year probation assistants?

	Absolute frequency	Percentage
Not applicable	9	50.0
Annually	1	5.6
Fortnightly	1	5.6
Weekly	1	5.6
No response	6	33.3

Table 4.10 How often do assistant chiefs supervise assistants with more than two years' experience?

	Absolute frequency	Percentage
Not applicable	9	50.0
Annually	1	5.6
Monthly	3	16.7
No response	5	27.8

confirmation that increases assistant chief probation officer involvement. Even so, it may be of interest to note the extent to which
chief officer grades are formally supervising field staff which must
have 'spin off' advantages in terms of understanding issues at grass
roots level.

With the growth of administrative staff in the service and their developing role it is important to consider the supervision of administrative staff. It may well be worthy of a separate piece of research in its own right as the very term administrative staff is vague and in our service can cover an extraordinary wide range of tasks. Of course the service employs a considerable number of secretaries and in more recent years the senior secretary or office supervisor has emerged. Also professional administrators are now firmly established in most services but not always clearly fitting the line management system in terms of supervision. But what about the development of specialist posts? For example, does an information and research officer count as administrative back-up, and who should supervise? Who has the skills to offer meaningful support and guidance? These are questions well beyond the scope of this piece of work which is essentially concentrating on the supervision of practice in the service. However the topic has been included in a small way in the hope that it will assist in getting it on agendas elsewhere! The only grade that was asked to comment on the supervision of administrative staff was assistant chiefs, and Table 4.11 emerged.

Table 4.11   How often do you regularly supervise administrative staff?

	Absolute frequency	*Percentage*
Not applicable	6	33.3
Never	2	11.1
Monthly	3	16.7
Fortnightly	1	5.6
Weekly	1	5.6
No response	5	27.8

This response suggests there are considerable grey areas regarding administrative staff. The 'not applicable' and 'no response' total 61.1 per cent, which leaves us to ponder the possibility that other grades are carrying out the supervision or perhaps it is not being done. Presumably the positive responses related to senior administrative staff and/or personal secretaries.

Overall, the vast majority of staff at all levels are receiving supervision. Perhaps not everybody is able to obtain the amount of time they would like from the supervisors and although this state of affairs occasionally leads to criticism, it does also suggest that staff are positive about the concept of supervision and that it is potentially valuable for all concerned. There is agreement at all levels that 'supervision is both desirable and necessary for the protection of clients and workers' and that 'supervision ought to occur and be adequate to the needs of all grades'.[1] The reasons why at present we cannot always meet this aspiration will be discussed later, but the dilemma is encapsulated by this quote from a senior probation officer: 'Due to other pressures I find I can't achieve the standards I set myself'.

Objectives of supervision

As described earlier in Chapter 1, the objectives of supervision have already shifted emphasis on a number of occasions. During the service infancy supervision was seen as essentially a supportive, at times banner-waving exercise. Later an inspectorial element was introduced. The 1950s and 1960s saw the growth of the supervisor as casework consultant, a role which has been in decline during the 1970s and 1980s. As field staff have developed their skills as caseload managers in recent years, seniors have been moving towards the role of resource managers.

It is difficult to assess to what extent these developments are genuine shifts in emphasis as opposed to merely adding objectives to the general heading of supervision. It is vital that there be clarity about this as clearly a supervisor who merely adds these developments to the existing task will eventually become hopelessly overworked or dilute each component to a level that is unsatisfactory to all concerned. The assistant chief probation officer who feels he ought to be operating as a 'senior senior' vis-à-vis staff supervision, but also faced with many other demands in terms of service development, can easily be led down this road until eventually he is operating at a level that is unsatisfactory to all levels of the service. Very often people in this situation feel they have no time to stand back and assess with a constructive advisor what is happening, thus a vicious circle is perpetuated.

Tables 4.12–4.14 refer to the importance attached by field, senior and chief officer grades to ten supervision objectives. They are reassuring in that there is a high level of agreement as to the primary objectives of supervision. However, closer scrutiny reveals some cause for anxiety.

It can be seen that 'providing a second opinion in difficult situations' was ranked seventh by chief officers and eighth by seniors. However, field officers placed this objective much higher, in third place. This difference may well be related to the anxiety expressed several times during interviews regarding the role of the senior probation officer as a casework consultant. It seems that currently

Table 4.12 Objectives of supervision in order of importance — assistant chief officer responses

		Median figure[1]
1	Stimulating thought and widening horizons re service task	1.500
2	Facilitating professional development	2.750
3	Ensuring minimum standards of practice are adhered to	3.500
4	Ensuring staff accountability to the service	3.833
5	Opportunity for staff to share problems	4.500
6	Assessment of staff performance, material for staff evaluation	6.833
7	Provision of information for future planning by management	7.500
8	Provision of a second opinion in difficult situations	7.500
9	Identifying training needs	9.000
10	Protection against criticism should things go wrong	9.167

Table 4.13 Objectives of supervision in order of importance — senior probation officer responses

		Median figure[1]
1	Facilitating professional development	2.500
2	Stimulating thought and widening horizons re service task	3.071
3	Ensuring staff accountability to the service	3.170[2]
4	Ensuring minimum standards of practice are adhered to	3.500
5	Opportunity for staff to share problems	4.107
6	Identifying training needs	5.500
7	Assessment of staff performance, material for staff evaluation	5.667
8	Provision of a second opinion in difficult situations	6.250
9	Provision of information for future planning by management	7.000
10	Protection against criticism should things go wrong	7.800

Table 4.14 Objectives of supervision in order of importance — probation officer responses

		Median figure[1]
1	Stimulating thought and widening horizons re service task	2.077
2	Facilitating professional development	2.750
3	Provision of a second opinion in difficult situations	4.500
4	Ensuring minimum standards of practice are adhered to	5.000
5	Opportunity for staff to share problems	5.136
6	Identifying training needs	5.333
7	Ensuring staff accountability to the service	6.591
8	Assessment of staff performance, material for staff evaluation	6.955
9	Protection against criticism should things go wrong	7.833
10	Provision of information for future planning by management	8.553

Notes:

[1] Median figures obtained from computer analysis.
[2] Due to an error this objective was missed out in the senior probation officers' questionnaire. The median figure given was taken from the pilot study sent to ten senior probation officers. Therefore, it cannot be regarded as statistically sound as the other figures. This omission also accounts for the senior probation officer median figure being generally lower. They were ranking objectives from 1 to 9, not 1 to 10, as the other grades were required to do.

this role is out of fashion and seniors, particularly new seniors, are being advised to move away from this role. However, during interview chief officers were quite clear they did not wish this role to be terminated by seniors. It was said they should be 'Available for case-work consultancy'. On another occasion an assistant chief probation officer who had given the issue much thought and had a clear strategy with his senior group stated that the aim was to 'Reduce the quantity but improve the quality'.

However for some seniors this is not the message, or if it is they are not hearing it very clearly. They only seem to be hearing the easy part — reduce the quantity. This creates a different kind of stress related to anxiety about the lack of consultation and validation of work being carried out with an increasingly 'high risk' category of offender.

> They keep telling me I'm a manager but when something goes wrong they want to know about my supervision of that case with the officer.

It may be that seniors have ranked 'casework consultancy' eighth as this is the message they are hearing. They may well also be feeling rather uneasy about it.

Field staff obviously feel consultancy is an important facility. Many of those I spoke to recognised the need for better information systems, new innovations, improved co-ordination of resources, etc. Often they were sympathetic to the senior probation officer predicament. However, they felt there was a substantial gap which if not filled will slow down the professional development of new officers particularly. It was pointed out that CQSW courses only train staff to basic competence and that it was the responsibility of the agency to build on that. Furthermore there was always the fear of a 'Beckford' case exploding, revealing poor professional practice, poorly supervised. Statements such as:

> My senior is involved in the community, draws up charts and surveys, does a lot of monitoring — but I've only been around two years and there is lots I need to know and develop. I'd prefer the traditional model.

or

> Our seniors have moved away from casework consultancy — but somebody has to do it. It doesn't feel adequate to leave it with teams. There's not a strong enough formal framework. Management must take responsibility for ensuring that role is carried out.

were not uncommon amongst field staff. Perhaps the importance of

56

casework consultancy needs to be addressed at all levels in an effort to resolve the problem. What is it? How can it be addressed in a way that meets the needs of officers and can be validated by management?

A further question raised by the tables is the importance of accountability. Whilst it was seen as a fairly important factor by seniors and assistant chiefs this objective came a very poor seventh, well behind the identification of training needs, in the field staff table. At first sight this is surprising as all officers interviewed seemed to feel this was an important topic and accepted that field staff needed to be accountable for their actions. Indeed the National Association of Probation Officers East Midlands branch working party report recently reaffirmed that 'Monitoring and accountability'[2] is one of the three key elements of supervision. However, further discussion revealed that whilst many field staff feel that accountability is important, it should not be so closely bound up with supervision. Perhaps this is why field staff ranked 'Ensuring minimum standards of practice are adhered to' much higher in fourth position. They seem to be saying it would be better to be held to account by measurement against agreed standards of practice. If standards were agreed then the inspectorial role of line managers would be clearer and could be separated from supervision. This would allow supervision to focus more clearly on professional development unless the inspection of work presented problems of compliance with minimum standards. Some staff felt that a set of minimum standards might go further and illustrate the impossibility of their task unless more resources were obtained. For some, lack of resources surrounds supervision with a layer of hypocrisy.

Overall, it is encouraging to see the high level of agreement regarding the objectives of supervision. Given this agreement perhaps there is scope for clarification as to who and how these objectives can be met given the limited resources available to the service. However the list given in the questionnaires was by no means comprehensive. Many respondents added further objectives that demonstrate the complexity of the task.

Each item within Tables 4.15—4.17 can be seen as important. Trying to incorporate them all is a daunting task, but not impossible. There are plenty of positive comments made by the consumers of supervision. The words in the following quote may not sound complimentary, but the 'feel' certainly is: 'The area is pressured, demands sometimes unreasonable. My senior, God help her, is often used as a buffer.'

It may well be that the feelings colleagues have about each other and their situation is also a crucial factor. In the words of a senior probation officer following his/her ranking of the objectives of supervision: 'Overall atmosphere needs to be supportive, otherwise most of the above are theoretical pious hopes'.

Table 4.15   Additional objectives mentioned by field staff

	Times mentioned
Support	4
Permit efficient use of resources	3
Sharing of skills and experiences	2
Workload management	2
Constructive criticism	2
Feedback on performance	2
Coping with stress	2
Encouragement	2
Teaching	1
Forum for airing new ideas	1
Provision of basic information	1
Encouraging consistency of practice	1
The promotion of views to management	1

Table 4.16   Additional objectives mentioned by senior probation officers

	Times mentioned
Support	2
Keeping senior probation officer in touch	2
Identifies resource needs	2
Team development	1
Inspection	1
Developing self-awareness in staff	1
Motivating staff	1
Communicating policy issues	1
Setting objectives	1
Developing specialisms	1
Co-ordinating resources	1

Table 4.17   Additional objectives mentioned by assistant chief probation officers

	Times mentioned
Suggesting models of supervision for senior probation officers	1
Consultations	1
Motivating staff	1
Resource allocation	1
Support	1
Validation (giving meaning to professional self in absence of empirical evidence)	1
Personal development	1

The effects of supervision

Given the complexity outlined regarding the objectives of supervision it follows that the effects are likely to be wide ranging. Essentially supervision is a communication requiring a thinking, feeling or doing response. Therefore respondents were asked to comment on nine possible effects that were all linked to one of these responses. Respondents were limited in their expression regarding the impact of these nine effects to one of three possibilities — no effect, little effect, or a substantial effect. Figures 4.1—4.7 illustrate the effects respondents felt supervision has. The percentages given show adjusted frequency as there were a few returned questionnaires with no response to this question.

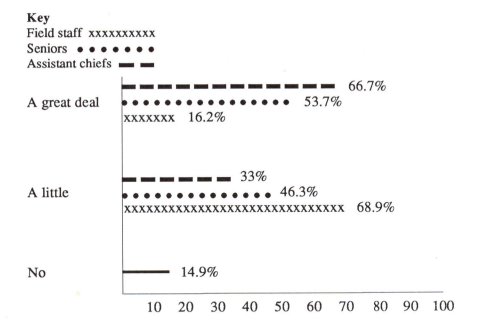

Figure 4.1   Does supervision improve your work?

It is clear that most people feel that supervision improves the quality of work undertaken, although seniors and assistant chiefs are rather more optimistic about the impact than field staff. Positive comments from field staff included constructive criticism, workload management discussions and the chance to influence agency policy, amongst other things. Such discussions were clearly seen as improving the quality of work and were endorsed by seniors who also mentioned possibilities such as encouraging staff to be more imaginative and the opportunities for shared learning. Some seniors acknowledge that officers can often be most helpful to them and their professional development. Chief officers' comments included the element of confidence-building and it was clearly felt that good supervision should give greater depth to practice.

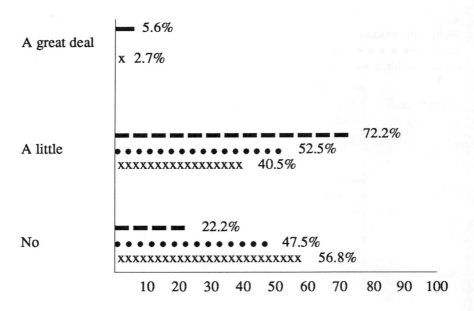

Figure 4.2   Does supervision place staff under more pressure?

We can see from Figure 4.2 that the largest percentage suggests a little pressure is added via supervision but nearly as many people felt no extra pressure was added at all. However, subsequent interviews enabled discussions about the quality of supervision to take place and this clearly has some effect on the pressure people felt from supervision. A number of people commented in questionnaires and interviews on the problems of going into an unprepared supervision session. Apart from the anxiety-provoking nature of such meetings they often achieve little and in this situation become a chore for those taking part. I quote an officer during an interview: 'I'm not very committed to it (supervision). It's like an added burden. There is no structure — it usually collapses 'cos there's no agenda given till the day.'

A different perspective was put forward by an assistant chief in interview. Talking about the greater awareness of the need for good supervision and its more rigorous nature, he commented: 'We don't hide people anymore'. The effect of this approach did, he felt, add considerable pressure to all concerned. It is to be hoped that he over-stated the situation when he said: 'A lot are struggling in quiet desperation, frightened of disciplinary procedures'.

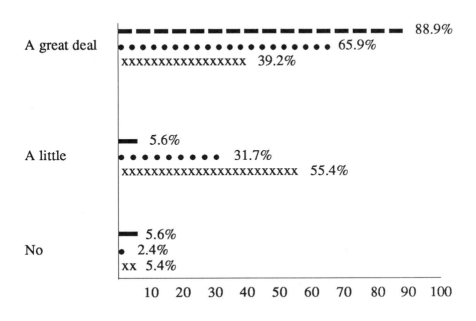

Figure 4.3   Does supervision help to clarify thinking?

The majority clearly feel that supervision does help to clarify thinking, although once again assistant chiefs are rather more optimistic about the impact than field staff. Nevertheless field staff did comment on the value of supervision for this end. The two quotes following summarise the feeling: 'Gives space to look at personal development and work', and 'Encourages me to stand back from my job from time to time and evaluate it and my own performance more objectively'.

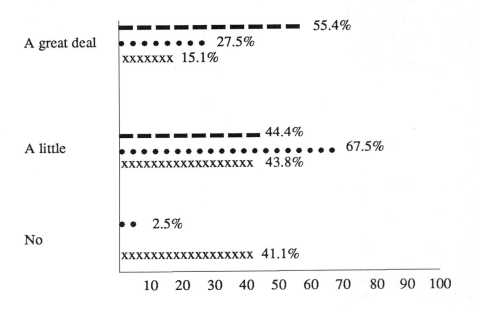

A great deal
  55.4%
  27.5%
  xxxxxxx 15.1%

A little
  44.4%
  67.5%
  xxxxxxxxxxxxxxxxx 43.8%

No
  2.5%
  xxxxxxxxxxxxxxxxxx 41.1%

10 20 30 40 50 60 70 80 90 100

Figure 4.4   Supervision makes me more enthusiastic

It seems that field staff do not feel supervision has much impact as a motivating force although seniors and assistant chiefs feel it has a considerable effect. Of course, many would want to respond to this question, 'it all depends on the quality of supervision'. The researcher wanted respondents to be free to answer from their own experience, good or bad, if they wished, whilst not denying that much will depend on the quality of supervision. A number of officers pointed this out, particularly more experienced staff who had suffered the morale-sapping experience of poor supervision and at other times the inspirational effect of excellent supervision.

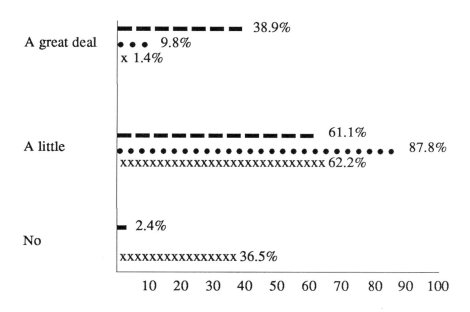

Figure 4.5   Can supervision change professional practice?

A very strong percentage was in favour of the view that supervision can influence professional practice, with once again field staff being rather more cautious about this than assistant chiefs. One of the difficulties with assessing such change is that the process is likely to be rather slow. Consequently many may feel that change is not taking place but after a decade look back and find they are virtually doing a different job from the one for which they were trained. The other problem is assessing to what extent supervision is responsible for change as opposed to changes in policy, resources, legislation etc. Bearing these things in mind many may well view Figure 4.5 as a considerable achievement for supervision.

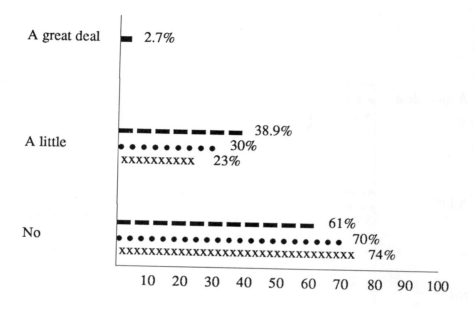

Figure 4.6   Does supervision have a depressing effect?

Most respondents did not see supervision as a depressing experience even though many commented on its challenge, the critical content, etc. This must be heartening for both supervisors and supervisees. It is perhaps surprising to find that nearly 40 per cent of chief officers feel supervision can have a depressing effect. It could be part of a general pattern of responses from chief officers that suggests they feel supervision has a powerful impact either positive or negative. However, an alternative view may be that they are sometimes called in to supervise on a 'trouble shooting' basis and this is likely to be a depressing experience.

Whilst analysing the data for this question a phenomenon appeared that the researcher had not previously considered. A number of respondents commented on the problems of changing supervisors. An officer interviewed talked about her depressing experience of supervision, much of which was attributed to regular changes in supervisor. 'During six years in the service I've had five supervisors. The effect has been catastrophic. I've been teaching them how to supervise me.' Another officer stated with great feeling: 'I've observed colleagues hammered by a change of supervisor'.

An assistant chief probation officer commenting on his experience of changing supervisors, mentioned the lottery element involved in the changes. He had experienced good and depressing supervision: 'My first senior probation officer was excellent, with the second I played the game. Later, when I went to . . . office I received no supervision at all!'

From the eighty-nine probation officers returning questionnaires a total of seventeen mentioned change of supervisor as having a substantial effect on their supervision. Of these, seven were non-committal as to the nature of the effect, five commented on a significant improvement and five felt very negative about the changes they had experienced. Remembering that line managers can have substantial power in terms of staff career prospects there may well be a case for further investigating the lottery element of supervisor/ supervisee relationships.

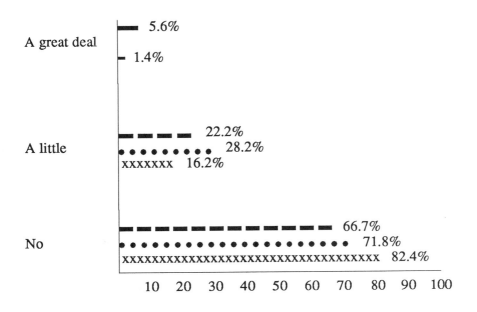

Figure 4.7   Does supervision encourage us to hide problems?

Once again it is heartening to see that for approximately three-quarters of the service, staff feel able to be open within the supervisory process. The minority that are not convinced there is openness linked their anxiety to the service evaluation process. As one senior probation officer put it: 'They won't bring their weaknesses to me — they know I'm part of the evaluation process'.

However it may be erroneous to lay too much importance on the evaluation process as the stumbling block to openness. After all, the 75 per cent who are not anxious about openness are also involved in this process. Analysis of interviews suggests that people may sometimes use the evaluation process as the reason for holding back when there are other more fundamental reasons, such as a personality conflict or conflict of outlook which has led to mutual distrust on a day to day basis. Obviously one of the end products of this distrust is likely to be tension surrounding the evaluation process, but this is not the same as claiming that the evaluation process itself is the problem.

Besides the effects specifically mentioned in the questionnaire, respondents identified many others. Assistant chief officers suggested the following may occur:

(a) Improved staff relationships
(b) Improved communications
(c) Improved confidence
(d) Improved co-operation
(e) Staff more willing to accept responsibility
(f) Shows staff their work is valued
(g) Reminds managers of 'coal face' problems and initiative
(h) Humanises the process of being managed
(i) Tests our perceptions
(j) Raises consciousness re core tasks
(k) Widens possibilities in the decision-making processes
(l) Officers' support.

Senior probation officers added the following:

(m) Reduces stress
(n) Demonstrates respect for staff
(o) Demonstrates professional nature of task
(p) Encourages sharing
(q) Encourages disciplined use of time.

The probation officer list included:

(i) Reducing stress
(ii) Helps senior probation officer

(iii) Exchange of knowledge
(iv) Enhances team identity
(v) Highlights training needs of senior probation officers
(vi) Gives a sense of common purpose
(vii) Opportunities for feedback on performance.

Overall the response suggests that for most people in the service supervision is a constructive, supportive experience and its effects are beneficial. There are difficulties and for those experiencing problems life becomes very stressful. Working in the probation service is stressful at all levels and the supervision process has been developed largely to help deal with stress. If the facility is not working it can easily add to stress, making the position almost intolerable for those working in it.

The effects of service changes in task, aims and practice

Chapter 1 on the history and development of staff supervision in the probation service demonstrates the degree and pace of change since 1907. Our target clientele, and our practice, are constantly being reviewed whilst the service itself has been growing in numbers since those early days. Sometimes there has been rapid expansion as in the 1960s, sometimes growth is very small, as has been the case so far during the 1980s. Whatever the current situation it will have implications for staff supervision. For example, during the 1960s the rapid growth brought with it the substantial problem of relatively in-experienced supervisors, supervising a very inexperienced workforce. This produced a challenge different from the current challenge to supervisors. What does today's supervisor have to offer the talented, experienced, committed staff we have now who are looking for challenge and professional development in a service that can provide few opportunities due to limited growth? We now have many experienced supervisors and supervisees with a new challenge regarding the direction of supervision.

The questionnaires asked respondents to comment on six developments within the service that are currently much talked about by its members. These were:

(a) The growing emphasis on working with 'high risk' offenders in the community.
(b) The growth of projects within the service and the degree to which staff are expected to develop projects.
(c) The changing roles of staff in the service.

(d) The growing emphasis on packages within probation orders that commit clients and staff to tighter contracts with courts.
(e) The movement towards teamwork approaches.
(f) The trend towards local statements of objectives and priorities.

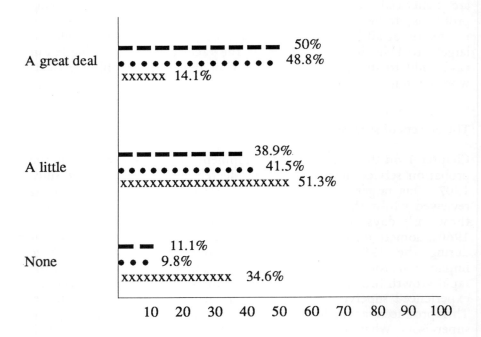

A great deal
▬ ▬ ▬ ▬ ▬ ▬ ▬ ▬ 50%
● ● ● ● ● ● ● ● ● ● ● ● 48.8%
xxxxxx 14.1%

A little
▬ ▬ ▬ ▬ ▬ ▬ ▬ 38.9%
● ● ● ● ● ● ● ● ● ● ● ● 41.5%
xxxxxxxxxxxxxxxxxxxxxxxxx 51.3%

None
▬ ▬ 11.1%
● ● ● 9.8%
xxxxxxxxxxxxxx 34.6%

10 20 30 40 50 60 70 80 90 100

Figure 4.8 **What effect is the growing emphasis on working with 'high risk' offenders in the community having on supervision?**

It can be seen that whilst a substantial group drawn from all grades feel this issue is affecting supervision a little, the remainder differ considerably depending on grade. Half of the chief officers and 48.8 per cent of seniors feel the issue is affecting supervision a great deal. However, a relatively small sample, 14.1 per cent of field staff agree with this assessment. During interviews there seemed little enthusiasm for this topic, unlike some of the others in this section, and I formed the overall impression that the substantial effect senior grades suggested may well be what they thought should be the case rather than what is. Several field staff pointed out that if working with high risk offenders in the community was cause for concern, surely this was a case for strengthening the casework consultancy role, not making it subordinate to the resource manager role.

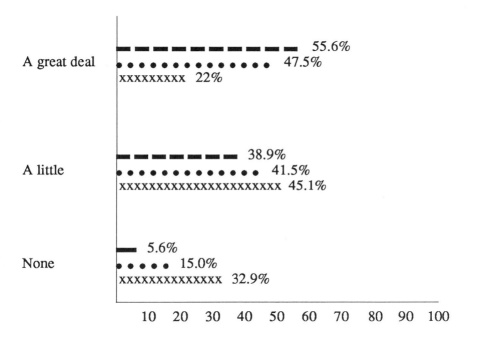

Figure 4.9 **What effect is the growth of projects within the service and the degree to which staff are expected to develop projects having on staff supervision?**

Figure 4.9 suggests similar feelings to those ascribed to the previous question. A large body of opinion feels the growth of projects has had a little effect but few field staff feel, as many senior grades do, that project work has had a significant impact. Once again the senior grades may have been commenting on what ought to be rather than what is.

This possibility is nicely illustrated by a field officer who wrote on his questionnaire:

> My change of role to day centre probation officer means I'm no longer able to fill time discussing problematic cases and no real effort has been made by myself or senior probation officer to reevaluate the purpose of supervision.

Interestingly, several respondents were involved in projects linked with other agencies which clearly required a review of the supervisory processes. When this had been carried out supervisees became very positive about their supervision:

> Experience working in a multi-agency setting necessitates a much broader view of the purpose and principles of supervision. Everything has become more open and the sense of sharing has been very important to me. As far as practice is concerned this suggests a separation of supervision from evaluation as a process.

However if a review is not carried out then life becomes very difficult for everyone and the quality of work suffers accordingly:

> A basic grade probation officer can have more than one supervisor with the possible further erosion of clarity and direction within the supervisory process.

It can be clearly seen (Figure 4.10) that not one of the assistant chief officers that returned questionnaires felt that changing roles had not affected the supervisory process, whereas 37.3 per cent of field officers felt role changes were not affecting supervision. This is the most dramatic difference in a table that suggests approximately 40 per cent feel there is some effect whilst the rest differ considerably depending on grade. It is perhaps not so surprising to see 37.3 per cent of field staff suggesting changing roles not making a scrap of difference. An assistant chief officer, discussing changing roles within the service, wryly commented: 'In broad terms we have become the policy makers and field staff are policy implementors. But in terms of determining priorities field staff still do as they want.'

During interviews the issue of policy-making was discussed on many occasions particularly the notion that chief officers were becoming policy makers, seniors were becoming policy monitors and field staff were becoming policy implementors. Certainly seniors commented regularly on the increased pressure to move their teams towards

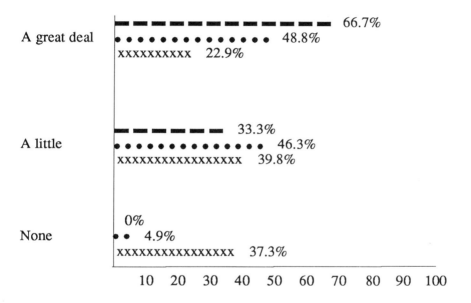

Figure 4.10   What effect are the changing roles
                of staff having on staff supervision?

targets set by chief officers. A senior probation officer described his
feelings:

> I'm a policy monitor. We even have competitions and league tables here.
> Chief officers are the policy makers although I do have a role. A strong team
> can respond to a strong chief probation officer. [In this conversation the
> senior probation officer was referring to his chief probation officer being
> firm with the Home Office.] We shared our views about day care this
> morning. We don't want custody in the community, we want day care based
> on the needs of clients in the community. That's where we're going.

The changing role of the senior probation officer seems to be causing some confusion at present. There is a strong lobby for senior probation officers to move from case consultancy to resource manager. However, with the growth of the service and the trend towards more clearly defined objectives and priorities many senior probation officers feel their discretion and scope as managers have been restricted. County objectives may well limit the degree to which a senior probation officer can respond to his field staffs' demands based on assessments of local needs and priorities. An assistant chief probation officer stated: 'The move of senior probation officers away from the senior practitioner role squarely into management has been the most significant role change.'

However, some senior probation officers question if this has really happened and even if it has, what their role is in management terms. Those I spoke to felt more like policy monitors whereas many field staff perceived the changing roles this way:

> They are too busy developing and don't get around to telling us when we've done well. A lot of my stuff is unspectacular but I have to put a lot of work in and it would be nice to be appreciated. You only seem to get noticed when your head's on the block.

An interesting development of role put forward by an assistant chief probation officer was described as: 'Part of the role of the assistant chief probation officer is to stop the excesses of the chief probation officer!'

Figure 4.11 shows that just over one-third of respondents of all grades took the middle line on the question of 'packages within probation orders'. The other two-thirds are in considerable disagreement, the difference between field staff and assistant chiefs being particularly noteworthy. Once again it could be argued that chief officers' answers reflect their desire rather than reality. It may well be true that no more new probation orders have extra conditions in them than in the 1970s. However, report-writing practice has been changing in recent years and there is an expectation that officers will be more specific with their plans for a client in the report if further intervention is envisaged. Presumably this is a focus of supervision in the 1980s and this may suggest that the chief officer assessment is accurate. Senior probation officers are fairly evenly distributed across all three bands which is a little alarming. Does this mean for some staff this topic is a regular feature for discussion in supervision whilst for others it is never mentioned? If so, this could lead to a patchy service to courts that the judiciary may well find confusing.

During interviews it emerged that few people were very interested in this question. It is difficult to know why. In at least two cases I

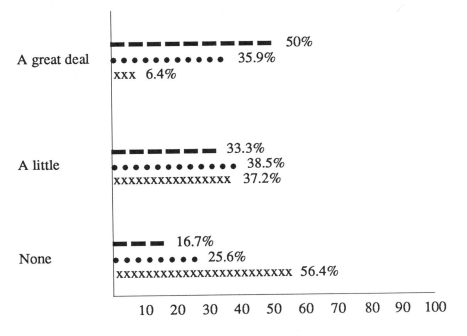

Figure 4.11 What effect is the growing emphasis on packages within probation orders that commit clients and staff to tighter contracts with courts having on the supervisory process?

was left with the impression that the interviewees were tired of talking about contracts and conditions having spent a lot of 1985 talking about them. These questions were framed that year and at that time 'schedule 11s', beefed up probation orders and the debate concerning the compulsory or voluntaristic nature of day care was in full swing. It may be that a year later these issues were burnt out, hence the relatively low interest. That is not to say these issues have been resolved but in many cases decisions have been taken and we must wait to see the results different approaches have.

The other possible reason for the lack of qualitative data is that in many cases the 'packages' referred to have led to the appointment of specialists. For these people this question is only one of a series of problems related to supervision and furthermore for them it is not a high priority problem. Specialists and supervision is looked at in detail in a later section.

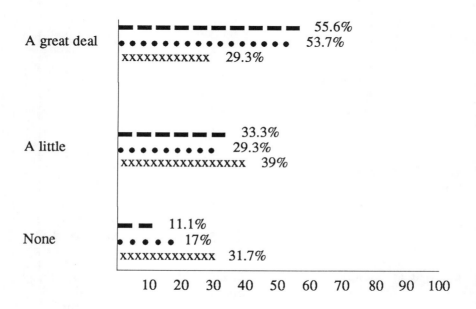

Figure 4.12   What effect is the movement towards teamwork approaches having on supervision?

There is rather more agreement regarding the effects of teamwork on supervisory processes than on previous questions. Also the responses are in the main positive. In fact field staff and seniors both recorded their highest percentages of answers in the top category for this section, 29.3 per cent and 55.6 per cent respectively. There were many positive statements linking teamwork with team supervision such as:

It tends to be a safe atmosphere. It can be very critical but this is positively undertaken. Team supervision provides more sharing and appreciation of colleagues and their differing methods of work plus an opportunity of influencing policy more constructively.

This comment came from a field officer in a team that is, incidentally, carrying out team evaluation, apparently with little difficulty. Positive comments were also made by assistant chiefs. It is important to note that assistant chiefs have been developing teamwork approaches with groups of seniors for some years now often with great success. Such developments have obvious benefits particularly for multi-team offices in the city areas. Reducing duplication and more efficient use of resources are obvious advantages. However, some seniors have recognised that there are also advantages for them in terms of professional development. As one senior probation officer put it the 'recognition of the role of peer group in supervision' can be very beneficial. However, it is clear that the recognition that teamwork has had a considerable impact on supervision should not be confused with the idea that everybody is agreed that team supervision is a good thing. Many people have extensive reservations. An assistant chief probation officer described the 'tyranny of the team' pointing out that adopting a teamwork approach does not put everybody 'on the way to freedom'.

Respondents from all grades expressed concern regarding the accountability component. Can a team take on the responsibility for its workload? Can a team be held accountable if things go wrong? Some seniors seem to see teamwork as a threat to their existence and are concerned about what was described to me as 'the attempt to separate supervision and consultation from management of the task'.

It is difficult to assess the impact of teamwork on supervision because there are so many differing views on what constitutes a teamwork approach. Even the simplest of teamwork functioning is not without its critics. A field officer describing an attempt to promote case discussions within a team stated: 'Moves towards more team supervision of casework have been resisted because this is moving towards the "managers" concept that has gained ground — a regressive step'. This is perhaps an understandable point of view if one is trying to defend the right to casework consultancy from your supervisor and you feel this facility is being disowned by management. However, it sadly denies the expertise and breadth of experience within a team and puts pressure on management to pretend there is such an animal as 'the omnipotent senior'. This fictitious beast can also be resurrected by other grades. An assistant chief probation officer unhappy with the notion of team supervision stated: 'I don't want to undermine the senior probation officer. People play games. You've got to try and reinforce the senior probation officer.'

Clearly many people feel that teamwork approaches are very powerful. Our knowledge of group dynamics makes us acutely aware of the power for good or evil of any group. Have we as a service the ability to harness the power of a teamwork approach to a positive direction? The feedback from this research suggests it can be done but there are no shortcuts. Many hours must be spent working out boundaries and issues of accountability. If an arrangement can be found it must be validated by management and a high level of trust is required. Perhaps one of the problems of teamwork is that the trust required can take months if not years to build, but this trust can be destroyed in minutes.

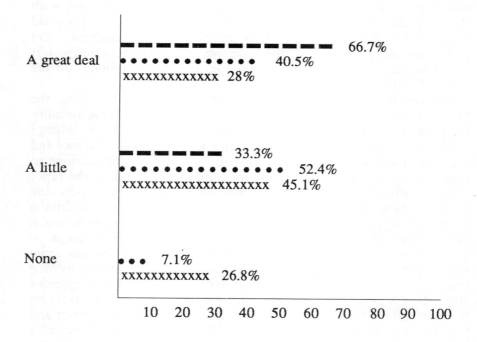

Figure 4.13   What effect has the trend towards local statements of objectives and priorities had on the
supervisory processes?

Most people feel local statements have affected staff supervision and a substantial grouping feel the supervisory processes have been affected a great deal. Following the pattern of this section, chief officers feel local statements have had a stronger impact than seniors feel, and seniors credit local statements with more impact than field staff. This is understandable as local statements of objectives and priorities based on the national statement have only been in existence in most services for two or three years. Therefore it seems reasonable to allow some time for their impact to percolate through the organisation. The figures suggest that assistant chiefs have been discussing local statements with seniors at some length but at present this may not have affected field staff much, perhaps no more than agreement on some team targets. However, in the next year or two it may be that field staff experience the impact of local statements on their supervisory process much more. Indeed there is evidence this is already happening. An officer working in an area with a well-developed local statement of objectives and priorities described his feelings during interview as: 'Supervision becomes providing information on how well we're doing in terms of the statement of local objectives and priorities'. Another field officer described the change in focus of his supervision sessions as follows: 'We now talk about fitting my caseload into the statement of local objectives and priorities rather than what my clients' needs are'.

These two comments suggest that their seniors have easily slipped into the policy monitoring role and it may be appropriate to suggest seniors be very aware of the seductive nature of this role. It has been mentioned earlier that local statements could push seniors into this role. Some seniors in interview have commented on their reduced ability to affect policy and are quite critical of the policy monitoring role. Field staff have been very critical of it. However, not all seniors are anxious. Some are very enthusiastic about the policy monitoring role. If the role becomes too pronounced the service runs the risk of developing with a one-way communication system — top down. The senior who sees the task as purely moving the team towards targets set and monitoring progress in this direction is likely to be of limited value to chief officer grades who want to know what new issues are around at field level and what initiatives field staff would like to put forward for meeting the constantly changing nature of service workload. Some assistant chiefs are aware of this danger. During interview one stated forcefully: 'Some seniors seem to think they have no other role than monitoring — setting up systems'.

In a stressful situation such as most people have to cope with in the probation service, policy monitoring could well become a safe place to hide. It is not necessary to produce new ideas — that is the chief officer's job. It is not necessary to put policy into practice — that is the field staff's task. The policy monitor can impassively move information up, down and around. This may well be acceptable for some seniors but it does not seem likely to enhance quality of service in the long term. The researcher was quite anxious on hearing a senior comment: 'I prefer the logistics rather than casework supervision'.

Assistant chiefs have been involved in a lot of work regarding the production of local statements and naturally they wish to see words turned into actions. However there is the possibility that having produced a local statement those closely involved become protective about it, wanting everything to have a clear link to it and reluctant to review it. It was pointed out by an assistant chief that this may well have already happened to a degree when the original statement of national objectives and priorities was produced. The strong, alert service management accepted it as a discussion starter and amended it to meet local needs. However, some managements only tinkered with it and may still be reluctant to thoroughly review it three years later. This reluctance to call on all information available before producing a local statement leaves field staff feeling suppressed and encourages a stagnant reactive attitude to supervision. An assistant chief described his thoughts:

> The statement of national objectives and priorities has given some chief probation officers managerial guts for the first time and some are hiding behind it. The good ones were already doing it but we need more collective responsibility for collective efforts. Managements should set objectives for themselves when they review the statement of local objectives and priorities.

Management must look hard at the way their communication systems, particularly the supervisory processes, have been affected by the statement of national objectives and priorities and the statement of local objectives and priorities. It would be easy for a management to avoid this by convincing itself it was one of those that had thoroughly reviewed the statement of national objectives and priorities and produced a local statement that was tailored to meet local demands. If this is so, why do many local statements of objectives and priorities look so startlingly similar?

The position of specialists was referred to several times in questionnaires in relation to local statements. Obviously local statements are only a brief outline regarding a service's plans for the coming year. Nevertheless they are seen as an indicator of the importance or otherwise of different aspects of our task by staff, committees and other interested bodies. The position of the specialist is often a difficult and isolated one especially if it is a developmental post. What message do managements give therefore to supervisors and supervisees if no mention is made of a specialist activity in a local statement? An officer, very committed to an innovative project stated flatly: 'We were barely mentioned in our statement of local objectives and priorities'. This may seem a small point but the officer felt this to be another powerful indicator that the service had little interest in their work. It becomes difficult for anybody to be motivated within the supervisory process in this situation.

Besides commenting on the items mentioned in the questionnaire many respondents put forward other suggestions which they felt had an effect on the supervisory processes. They included the following:

1   *Field officer suggestions*
    (a)   The length of time in the job
    (b)   Environmental and emotional issues in the workplace
    (c)   Shared working (e.g. prison officers/probation officers)
    (d)   Developing community involvement
    (e)   The small sub-office
    (f)   A more directive approach by some seniors
    (g)   Change in supervisor ('Our senior retired recently, during her time at the office supervision was non-existent. We have acquired a new senior who is the opposite. The team are feeling like incompetent students.').

2   *Seniors' suggestions*
    (a)   Increase experience of field staff
    (b)   Increase of political perception of client/community
    (c)   New legislation (New officers seem to need more basic teaching.)
    (d)   Development of minimum standards
    (e)   Informal supervision.

3   *Assistant chief suggestions*
    (a)   Increased use of monitoring and information systems
    (b)   Higher public profile for the service
    (c)   Lack of promotion opportunities
    (d)   The need to use resources effectively
    (e)   Increased accountability of senior probation officers
    (f)   Financial management initiative.

In summary when looking at changes in service task, aims and practice the biggest factor seems to be the introduction of local statements of objectives and priorities. Project growth, changing roles and the development of teamwork are also seen as having made a significant impact. The move towards high risk offenders seems to be accepted and has had an effect but the process seems to have been so gradual that few people find it worthy of significant debate. Lastly there is the question of court contracts. Most field staff felt this to be irrelevant to supervision but three-quarters of senior grades disagree. It did not raise much enthusiasm when mentioned in subsequent interviews. The questions remain: Is it irrelevant? Are people tired of talking about it? What is happening in practice?

On all questions in this section chief officers felt changes within the service were having a considerable effect. On every question at least half of the sample said the effects had been substantial. Seniors were not so sure although the majority of respondents felt each of the issues raised produced some effect on supervision. Field staff felt all the issues mentioned produced some effect on supervision with the exception of tighter probation packages for which 56.4 per cent felt they had no effect and 37.2 per cent felt they had little impact. Generally field staff tended to have the view that all of the issues in this section produced only a small impact on supervision.

Who is involved in the supervisory process?

Traditionally within the probation service supervision of staff has operated via the line management system. However, as the range of tasks has grown and service responses have developed the supervisory processes have to some extent been reviewed. Whilst line management supervision is still standard practice there are now many variations of this theme, some successful, others leading to confusion. The difficulty stems from the efforts of staff at all levels to find a process that will best meet all the components of supervision, a huge task if we accept Payne and Scott's view that 'All supervisory models will be unique'.[3] A statement made at the 1985 East Midlands conference of staff supervision illustrates the dilemma that field staff and managers face: 'Staff do need to reflect on their work but not necessarily with their managers. However, the manager must ensure the option to reflect is available.'[4]

Tables 4.18—4.20 illustrate the extent to which supervision has diversified from the classic line management system for each of the three grades researched.

It can be seen from Table 4.18 that 70 per cent of respondents receive the classic line management approach. Bearing in mind that 25 per cent either did not respond or do not receive supervision anyway, it seems fair to say that the classic approach is almost entirely

Table 4.18 Who is involved in your supervisory process?
(Assistant chief officers)

	Absolute frequency	Relative frequency in %
My CPO	10	50
My DCPO	4	20
I do not receive supervision	3	15
Outside consultants	1	5
No response to question	2	10
Total	20	100%

accepted at chief officer level. It seems likely that the one respondent who indicated supervision by outside consultant is reviewing progress regularly with the chief probation officer. No respondent mentioned an element of sharing their supervisory process with other assistant chief probation officer colleagues or their senior probation officer groups. Perhaps this lack of sharing via the supervisory process contributes to the fairly common situation in which assistant chief probation officer divisions within a service differ considerably. During interviews it was mentioned on a number of occasions that assistant chief probation officer divisions often operate as if they were mini-probation services in their own right. Greater sharing of thinking, experiences, problems, etc. may help to break down these boundaries and an element of shared supervision would seem a logical step assuming an acceptable level of trust exists. If not this would need to be remedied before shared supervision could be attempted.

Table 4.19 Who is involved in your supervisory process?
(Senior probation officers)

	Absolute frequency	Relative frequency in %
My ACPO	36	82.0
My ACPO and my team	4	9.1
I do not receive supervision	2	4.5
My ACPO and SPO colleagues	1	2.2
My CPO	1	2.2
Total	44	100.0%

When looking at the figures for seniors the percentage receiving classic line management supervision is even higher at 84.4 per cent. However, 11.3 per cent are diversifying and sharing their development with either senior colleagues or members of their team. In all these situations the assistant chief remains involved. During interviews one senior talked of his supervisory arrangement which allowed for line supervision and a senior probation officer support group which was involved in the senior probation officer evaluation process, although the assistant chief probation officer remains the author of the final evaluation document.

On most occasions those involved in group supervision at whatever level spoke positively about the experience, but there are problems. The main difficulty surrounds the appropriate level of openness and frankness. Some comments made suggested a frustration at the lack of openness, such as 'We can't come up with more than bland statements'. Others pointed out the dangers of blunt comments in a group situation: 'It is tempting to use experienced staff as consultants but this can be divisive'. This suggests a need for care when contemplating a widening of the supervisory process. Why is this being done? What areas do we expect people to comment on? What are the boundaries? Is there a sufficiently healthy atmosphere? If not, how can this be created?

Table 4.20   Who is involved in your supervisory process? (Field staff)

	Absolute frequency	Relative frequency in %
My SPO	52	60.3
I do not receive supervision	13	15.1
My SPO and my team	12	14.0
My team	2	2.3
My SPO and a colleague	2	2.3
My ACPO	1	1.2
My team and a colleague	1	1.2
My SPO and ACPO	1	1.2
My SPO, my ACPO and a colleague	1	1.2
My SPO, my team and an outside consultant	1	1.2
Total	86	100.0%

It can be seen from Table 4.20 there is substantially more diversification of the supervisory process. Only 62.7 per cent receive classic line management supervision, still a large number, but this leaves 22.2 per cent of respondents involved in a process which involves contributions from people outside the line. It is also clear that the service is developing a range of responses to meet the needs of individual staff.

The strongest development outside the line management system is obviously the element of team supervision. Fifteen officers (17.5 per cent) made it clear they were involved in such a process, normally with the senior probation officer taking part. It emerged from interviews that much of the move towards team supervision can be attributed to the growing number of specialist teams within the service and service policy of moving senior probation officers into these teams on secondment for a few years. This situation places the incoming senior in a task that often he/she knows little about whilst those already there have developed skills and knowledge regarding the team's task. A senior probation officer explained his response to that situation as follows:

> I needed to develop my knowledge of the team's work before I had anything to offer. Therefore we adopted a team approach to supervision. They set objectives and reviewed progress. I backed them up. I became a resource coordinator.

However this senior ran into difficulties at a later stage.

> I later received criticism for lack of individual supervision. I had failed to get the system validated by management. Then when staff disagreed with evaluations they quoted the lack of individual supervision.

An important message here. All systems need to be validated by management. However, one wonders why in this case team supervision did not extend to team evaluation. Were the team not prepared to 'own' their progress or otherwise? Team evaluations have been attempted on a number of occasions but seem to collapse within a short time, sometimes because key people move on, in other situations the process just seems to peter out. One probation officer described it: 'Team supervision means the whole team should be involved. It should include team evaluations but this was mysteriously dropped last year.' The two respondents who mentioned seniorless team supervision both pointed out that this was not by design. However, both have found the process constructive.

For many people the traditional supervision from a senior probation officer on a one to one basis is a most helpful exercise. A number of examples have been mentioned previously of field staff wanting to retain the traditional consultancy model. Also this style provides confidence in the worker that their work is approved of in terms of accountability, a grey area in some of the other arrangements. However, there are also comments which suggest field staff frustration with the traditional model and further comments that suggest a degree of collusion between senior probation officer and probation officer: 'I like my cosy chats'.

In summary there seems to be little sharing within the supervisory process amongst colleagues. Nearly all that is being done is at field level and some of these arrangements are not at all clear and could run into difficulties when a dispute emerges. Those that are involved in diversified supervision usually find the process helpful. It may well be worth more people giving the possibilities some thought so long as they do not fall prey to the 'good idea' syndrome.

Supervision reviews

Given the speed with which the service has been changing it is to be hoped that the supervision of staff being provided is developing to cope with the changes. Therefore the questionnaires sent to all

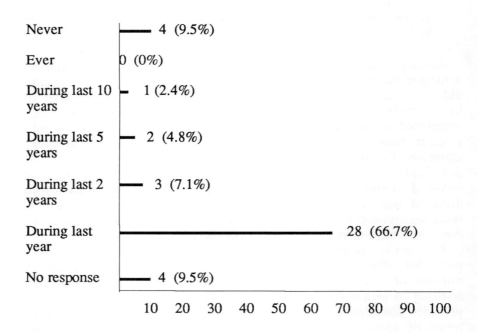

Figure 4.14   When was the team's supervisory process
last reviewed? Senior probation officer response

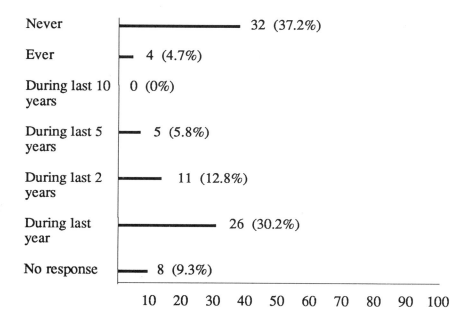

Never	———————— 32 (37.2%)
Ever	— 4 (4.7%)
During last 10 years	0 (0%)
During last 5 years	— 5 (5.8%)
During last 2 years	—— 11 (12.8%)
During last year	——— 26 (30.2%)
No response	— 8 (9.3%)

10 20 30 40 50 60 70 80 90 100

Figure 4.15   When was the team's supervisory process last reviewed? Field officer response

grades had a section related to the extent to which the supervisory processes were being reviewed. There were questions concerning how often reviews took place and who was involved. Let us first look at the extent to which supervision is on the agenda in a general sense before addressing the extent to which individuals have their personal supervisory process revised. Figures 4.14 and 4.15 are concerned with the extent to which all grades review the general supervisory processes within a team rather than individuals within a team. Seniors and field staff were asked to state when, if ever, the last review of supervision concerning the whole team was carried out. The seniors' questionnaire carried a further question asking for information as to who was involved in the review (Table 4.21).

It can be quickly seen that senior officers feel that reviews of team supervision are carried out more frequently than field staff feel they are. To some extent this discrepancy can be understood when we look at who is involved in this process. Obviously senior probation officers are key figures when reviewing the supervisory processes of a team. Only 9.5 per cent of seniors say they have at no time reviewed the processes within their team. However, what is meant by a review? Is it simply a chat with the assistant chief or are we talking about full-blooded, large-scale, county-wide initiatives requiring all levels to give thought to the matter? When seniors were asked to say who was involved in their reviews of team processes the answers were as follows:

Table 4.21   Who was involved in your review?

	Absolute frequency	Frequency as %
My chief probation officer	1	2.4
My assistant chief probation officer	17	40.5
My team	30	71.4
My SPO colleagues	9	21.4
The Home Office	2	4.8
Other outside consultants	3	7.1

It can be seen from Table 4.21 that in nearly 30 per cent of team supervision reviews, the teams concerned were not involved. This could account for field staff's much lower response when asked to say when reviews had taken place. They may not have known about them!

Despite the discrepancy between the two grades it can be seen that over 40 per cent of staff report a review within the last two years which suggests the service is becoming aware of the need to refine supervision to meet changing demands.

The figure of 40.5 per cent of team reviews involving chief officer grades may give cause for concern. New processes that have not involved senior management or even worse have not even been validated by them, may well prove lacking at the very times they are needed. Hopefully in the large percentage of cases that did not involve senior management representatives in the review, at least the outcomes will have been agreed by them.

The low percentage of reviews that included other senior probation officers is also disappointing. One would have thought that when reviewing processes there would be much to be gained from consulting with colleagues with a similar task. The need for sharing at senior probation officer level would be particularly strong in the multi-team officers where a change in process may have a 'knock on' effect concerning other teams.

As well as team reviews, all respondents were asked to state when they were last involved in a review of their personal supervision process, if ever. Field staff responded as follows:

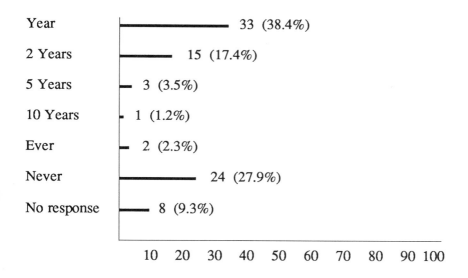

Figure 4.16   Has your supervisory process been reviewed during the last . . .

Figure 4.16 could be interpreted as an upsurge of interest during the last two years for most people, but leaving a worrying 27.9 per cent involved in a rather sterile process. However, this interpretation could be wrong. Much depends on whether staff feel that the initial arrangement they make could be called a review. Also very importantly how long have those who responded been probation officers? For example if half those who returned questionnaires were officers in the first three years of their careers it would send the percentage of 'never reviewed' artificially high.

With regard to the first issue field officers were asked during interview to expand on this question. Nobody had included their initial supervision arrangement as a review. With regard to the second matter — the length of service respondents had — Table 4.22 may be helpful.

Table 4.22   Probation officer respondents'
            length of time in post

	Actual frequency	*As a %*
10+ years	37	43.0
5–10 years	26	30.2
3–5 years	9	10.5
1–3 years	12	14.0
Less than 1 year	2	2.3
Total	86	100.0

We can see that 73.2 per cent of respondents had been serving probation officers for five years or more, 43 per cent for more than ten years. Therefore, it looks likely that many experienced staff have never been involved in reviewing the supervision they receive, even though their needs as a first-year officer are likely to be very different from that of an experienced member of staff undertaking a degree of specialisation, or possibly trying to cope with 'burn out', a phenomenon that is said to occur sometimes with experienced officers. Of the thirty-seven officers who had over ten years' experience within the survey, twenty-seven said they had reviewed their supervision, eight had never done so, and two felt the question was not applicable due to breaks in length of service. These figures suggest that the figure of 27.9 per cent never reviewing their supervision revealed in Figure 4.16 is fairly accurate, a worrying situation, particularly if the percentage 'holds up' when looking at officers with ten years or more experience, and this sample suggests it would.

During interviews field staff were encouraged to talk about the development of their supervision as their careers developed. The pattern that emerged suggested that new entrants received considerable supervision on a casework consultancy/accountability basis. However, within a few years the quantity of supervision was reduced and its purpose became increasingly vague. As one officer put it: 'For the first three years my supervision was excellent, but after that I started to outgrow my supervision in terms of quality'. Another officer commented: 'My first senior was all about accountability and that was OK for a first year officer. Unfortunately my senior probation officer now assumes that I'm still OK — but I'm not.'

Both these officers had more than five years' experience and their responses suggest a worrying situation. During the next few years due to no growth we are likely to be faced with more experienced officers looking to develop their field work skills than ever before. They are likely to be well qualified talented people. This is a real challenge for supervisors who will need to develop their skills in order to provide challenging, stimulating supervision. During interviews representatives of both senior and assistant chief grades acknowledged the need to review supervisory processes. The danger is that these reviews simply conclude that the amount of supervision can now be reduced as the officer has proved competent and trustworthy. Seniors becoming threatened by the abilities of their experienced staff can easily become timid, preferring to reduce quantity rather than meet the challenge of improving the quality.

Moving on to senior probation officers, they too were asked to state when their personal supervision process was last reviewed and who was involved. The results were as follows:

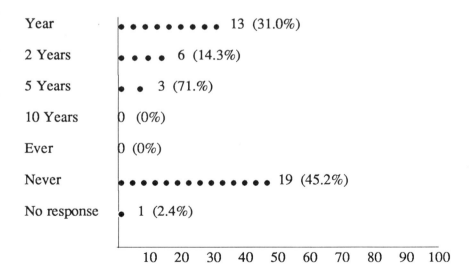

Figure 4.17   The supervision I receive has been
               reviewed during the last . . .

Table 4.23 Who was involved in your review?

	Absolute frequency	Frequency as %
My chief probation officer	3	7.1
My assistant chief probation officer	21	50.0
My SPO colleagues	6	14.3
My team	4	9.5
The Home Office	0	0.0
Other outside consultants	2	4.8
No response	6	14.3
Total	42	100.0

The figure of 45.2 per cent never having reviewed their personal supervision is even more worrying than the 27.9 per cent figure recorded by field staff. Once again the same reservations about the accuracy of this figure could apply. Is the figure high because a large percentage of the sample are fairly new appointments for whom a review is not yet appropriate? Unfortunately close inspection reveals a slightly worse situation. If we simply look at seniors with more than five years' experience we find that 24 out of the 42 respondents fit this category. Of the 24, 11 had reviewed their supervision, 12 had not, 1 not applicable.

Half the seniors with more than five years' experience have never reviewed the supervision they are experiencing despite the speed with which the service is developing and the changing needs of staff at various points in their careers. No doubt some would argue that the process of supervision is a form of constant review, but surely it would be helpful to stand back from the process and examine what is going on, the objectives, the priorities, etc. a little more often than we seem to be doing.

Looking at who is involved in the reviews (if they take place) we can see that common practice is to involve the assistant chief. If we add the 50 per cent in which assistant chiefs are involved to the 45.2 per cent in which reviews have not taken place we can see it is very rare for a review to take place of senior probation officer supervision without assistant chief probation officer involvement. We can also see that rarely do senior probation officer colleagues (14.3 per cent) or teams (9.5 per cent) have an opportunity to play a part in this process, although it seems likely that these groups may well be able to put forward some constructive suggestions in these situations. Of course such openness would require a good degree of trust but is this not a prerequisite of good management anyway?

It is interesting to compare Table 4.23 with the earlier Tables concerned with team reviews. It seems seniors are much happier to involve teams in a review of the team supervisory process than in a review of their personal supervisory needs. Understandable in many ways, but as the professional development of the senior probation officer is likely to be so vital to the development of the team is it really so important to separate them?

In interview, seniors regularly expressed their concern regarding their supervision and its direction. One problem mentioned several times was the different approaches of assistant chiefs, particularly if a senior is moving to different branches of the service every two or three years. It was said that assistant chiefs often had very different ideas as to what supervision should be, evaluation procedures and basically the criteria for good practice. It was said that despite protestations to the contrary: 'Assistant chiefs still operate as super seniors'. Another difficulty seemed to be time. As seniors and similarly assistant chiefs, felt their workloads had increased, it was easy for reflection on the purpose of supervision to be squeezed out. A senior probation officer pointed out: 'If we can't get our evaluations done on time what chance is there of reviewing our supervision processes?'

But what about assistant chiefs? Is it true 'that chief officer grades supervise each other in a fairly egalitarian way?'[5] Tables 4.24a and 4.24b show the response.

Table 4.24a   Have you reviewed your supervisory process during the last . . .

	Absolute frequency	Frequency as %
Year	14	70.0
2 years	4	20.0
5 years	2	10.0
10 years	0	0.0
Ever	0	0.0
Never	0	0.0

This looks much more of a planned process.

Table 4.24b   Who is involved in these reviews?

	Absolute frequency	Frequency as %
My CPO	6	30.0
My DCPO	1	5.0
My ACPOs	5	25.0
My SPOs	12	60.0
My field teams	5	25.0
The Home Office	1	5.0
Outside consultants	1	5.0
No response	1	5.0

The figures do seem to suggest a more egalitarian approach. Whereas the other two grades suggest that reviews are mostly carried out with superiors, only 35 per cent of assistant chiefs have involved line superiors in a review of their supervision. It may be that there was some ambiguity in the question that has distorted the figures. Although the question referred to 'your supervisory process' some assistant chiefs may well have taken this to mean the process they give rather than the one they receive. But even if this is the case it does suggest a willingness to share with subordinates to a degree well beyond that of senior probation officers. We can see that 60 per cent of assistant chiefs have talked with their senior probation officers about supervision, whereas when senior probation officers reviewed their supervision only 9.5 per cent consulted with the probation officer grade below.

However, there must be some anxiety about the way in which so many of these reviews are being carried out without reference to the chief probation officer or assistant chief probation officer colleagues. It does suggest once again that assistant chief probation officer divisions often behave as 'mini services' in their own right, developing policies and criteria without too much regard for developments in other divisions. One would have thought that a thorough review often involving senior probation officers as suggested in Table 4.24b was worth sharing with colleagues. This actually happens, if these figures are correct, in only 1 review in 4.

During interviews it was pointed out that the term review is vague. Does a note from a chief probation officer asking that suitable arrangements be made regarding staff supervision constitute a review? The answer is likely to depend on the recipients of the note. Some assistant chiefs receiving such a request might instigate a thorough check of proceedings and suggest improvements whilst another may do nothing more than push the request further down the line suggesting perhaps that senior probation officers ensure supervision is carried out. Tables 4.24a and 4.24b suggest that assistant chiefs are regularly reviewing their supervisory processes but not always sharing these reviews outside divisional boundaries. Perhaps chief officers could encourage more sharing of these reviews and their findings in order to develop better and more consistent practice.

Supervision of specialists

Many of the questionnaires returned made comments regarding the position of specialists in the service and it is certainly true that we have more staff adopting specialisms in some form than ever before.

Some staff are expressing anxiety about the possibility of probation field work becoming a minority specialist activity! These developments have substantial implications for staff supervision which must be tackled. If we do not face up to the changing nature of our organisation we will have more specialists echoing the view of one interviewed who stated quite simply: 'Nobody knows what to do with us'.

Because specialists and specialisms have very different problems, with implications for organisational change for those individuals struggling to cope with the problem, a separate piece of research was carried out. This involved sending a questionnaire to ten specialists asking their views as to the type of organisation they felt they were operating in (Appendix 6). These were followed up with interviews using an *aide memoire* (Appendix 7). The purpose of this research was:

1 To look at the processes that lead to the creation of a specialism.
2 Look at the effects of these decisions on practitioners and to obtain a practitioner's view of the objectives of these specialisms. How well supervised and supported are they, how is the task being monitored and what effect is the task having on them as individuals?
3 What does this mean for the future? Does the service feel that specialisation is effective? Are adjustments needed in the planning and supervision of specialisms?

Types of specialism

It is necessary to fully explore the meaning of the terms specialist and specialisms as they are applied to the service, as so much of the developments in these areas are, or began as, informal grassroots initiatives which were later legitimised by service management. The terms specialist or specialism have been used a great deal with users having widely differing thoughts as to their meanings. A further complication is that the service does create full-time specialist posts with fairly clear line management accountability whilst in other situations the specialist or specialism has 'evolved', leading to more complicated systems of supervision.

Firstly the service has had for years full-time specialists created as a result of managements recognising that there is a task to be undertaken which requires special expertise and which in itself constitutes a full-time occupation. A good example of this is the Crown Court Liaison Officer, an established post in most services in the country. The officers are officially recognised, there are clearly laid down tasks which must be carried out and the postholder is clearly accountable for the quality of work to a manager in the line management system. Clearly a task specialism. Other examples would include administration and training officers.

Another category of specialism that needs to be acknowledged is by group of clients or type of client. Many services have acknowledged ethnic minority officers, although the amount of space provided for the postholders to develop specialist expertise is variable between counties. The initial suggestion that this specialism be developed came from a Home Office circular,[6] but the development of expertise has in many counties been left to field teams to tackle on an informal basis. There are other examples of specialism by group or types of clients. For example, intermediate treatment workers identifying juvenile offenders as a client group.

A third manner of developing specialist expertise is via social work method. The service has for many years sent people on courses in certain areas of professional practice, such as counselling skills, groupwork skills, Heimler and transactional analysis. Occasionally members of staff have pursued a method of working and by agreement with colleagues moved towards a bias in their caseloads which enable them to use these methods.

Fourthly, the service allows specialisms to develop as a grassroots response to client need. By their nature these specialisms evolve and reflect the environment we are working in. At present with approximately four million people unemployed and a disproportionate number of these committing offences, the service is responding by developing day-care expertise and in some instances appointing specialists to work in day centres.

Many parallels regarding the development of specialists and specialisms can be drawn with social service departments. This is particularly true when comparing probation field teams and social service area teams. With this group of workers we are usually talking about individuals pursuing a specialism, a form of advanced general practice. In 1978, Bromley reserved the word specialist

For those whom we might otherwise regard as experts. These are the workers who are not only knowledgeable about the field in which they are concentrating, but have acquired a substantial knowledge which informs their professional practice and makes for a qualitative difference in the social work skills they possess. Such senior practitioners, 'experts' in whatever field, may be the only workers who are able to claim that label, by virtue of a substantial amount of practical experience. They will be the social work equivalent of the medical consultant.[7]

Organisational change

It is important for the probation service as an organisation to acknowledge not only the different types of specialism we are undertaking, but the growth of specialisms, the manner in which these areas of work are growing and what this means in terms of managements coping with the stresses and demands that will be made on it. For example, ten years ago many services had crown court, administration, community service, prison and residential specialisms — five areas all clearly agreed by management and with acknowledged line management accountability. In a modern probation service these specialisms still exist but we also have others such as intermediate treatment, civil work, day care, accommodation, ethnic minorities and training specialisms. In fact an explosion of specialisms, not all with clear line management accountability. Some projects have a short life, often we are dependent on enthusiasm and initiative and, further, the objectives of these specialisms may not be agreed. Other specialisms are emerging such as research workers, reparation units, through-care specialists, welfare rights specialists or specialists with women clients.

Lastly when considering the nature of specialists in the service we must acknowledge the different structure the organisation has used to acquire specialists. Many of the established specialists' posts are filled by secondment, usually for two or three years. However, there are others who hold permanent posts which could mean that if the postholder fails he or she may remain in that position until they retire! Thirdly there are the field initiative specialisms, whose terms of reference are often determined by the senior probation officer and/or the field team. Hopefully, these are at least validated by senior management.

Organisation management system

Clearly the development of specialisms in the service so far has been a complex combination of management and field staff initiatives. This state of affairs seems likely to continue, therefore in my opinion the organisation must give some thought as to how it can best supervise these developments. To do this requires some understanding of the organisation and how it functions. Firstly it seems right to say that a probation service is a bureaucratic organisation. This is not a disparaging remark, it is bureaucratic using Weber's indicators. It has:

(a) A continuous organisation of official functions bound by rules;
(b) A specified sphere of competence;

(c) The organisation of offices follows the principle of hierarchy;
(d) Specialised training is necessary and staff have to qualify for professional positions;
(e) Members of staff are separated from means of production or administration;
(f) Most policies, rules, decisions, are in writing;
(g) Legal authority can be exercised.[8]

Having established that using Weber's criteria the service is largely a bureaucratic organisation it is necessary to establish how specialisms can fit constructively into such an organisation. It is worthy of note at this stage that whilst the organisation may have many of the features associated with a classic bureaucracy it still gives a great deal of professional discretion to its fieldworkers. This means that decisions concerning the creation of a specialist task and the objectives behind the creation of specialist roles can be substantially undermined, or even ignored, if field staff do not have a commitment to them. So how can such an organisation establish specialisms in a constructive manner? We must, I think, understand the motivation of members of the organisation and the style of communication the organisation uses. Firstly, using Douglas McGregor's 'Theory X and Y' behaviour. The traditional theorists' concept of human nature he called Theory X and it assumed:

(a) Most people have an inherent dislike of work.
(b) In consequence, they must be either coerced or bribed to put in sufficient effort for an organisation to function effectively.
(c) Most people do not want responsibility and prefer to be directed.

McGregor does not deny that some human behaviour in organisations can be explained in Theory X terms but he suggests that there is increasing evidence that much behaviour cannot be satisfactorily explained in this way and that an alternative theory, Theory Y, is required to account for it.

(a) Most people do not inherently dislike work. In fact 'the expenditure of physical and mental effort in work is as natural as play and rest'. If the circumstances are right, work can be experienced as deeply satisfying.
(b) If people are committed to the goals of an organisation they do not require external control to make them work.
(c) Commitment of the individual will be at its highest where his work satisfies his own needs for self-actualisation.

(d) Given appropriate conditions, people can learn to accept and seek responsibility.

(e) In traditionally-run enterprises the potential of most people is not being fully developed or used.[9]

It follows that an organisation built on Theory Y principles will seek to structure its work so that it is responsible, demanding and potentially satisfying. To achieve these ends management must emphasise the establishment of mutually supportive relationships aimed at enabling people to do their work, rather than aim to develop close direction and control.

Although in general terms probation service staff fit the Theory Y category, there are some important points to note regarding specialists. Firstly, whilst people may be primarily motivated by Theory Y when they begin their careers with the service, which does after all see itself as 'a caring profession', as people move up the line management structure parts of the Theory X formula may grow in strength, as specialisms are sometimes presented as a means of promotion. Secondly, Theory Y may be appropriate when talking about specialisms that stem from client need or style of work. However, some specialisms are seen as meeting organisational needs and are not popular tasks, indeed in some cases managements feel obliged to direct members of staff into certain specialist posts. Working in prisons or court liaison posts are sometimes seen in this way. Consequently the response from staff in these positions may be more towards Theory X and management procedures and supervision must reflect this situation.

It would seem that a bureaucratic organisation with a workforce that to a large extent fitted McGregor's Theory Y would run into difficulties if it supervised staff in an autocratic manner. Most members of the organisation would be interested in the goals of the service and the manner in which it moved towards these goals. An authoritarian regime may well suppress these views which would probably result in poor performance in the long term. Certainly specialist posts or specialisms created, whose goals and contribution to the service as a whole were not clear and agreed at all levels of the organisation, might well find a lack of co-operation in some areas. So what is the style of communication in the probation service? Perhaps more important what do members of the organisation perceive the style of communication to be? In an effort to establish this, ten members of the service were sent Likert's questionnaire regarding different management systems. Likert had four main categories:

System 1 — Authoritarian, exploitative
System 2 — Authoritative benevolent
System 3 — Consultative
System 4 — Participative

Likert would like to see all organisations moving towards System 4 but he also noted that members of an organisation wanted to know what system was operating even if it was System 1. He would say that an authoritative exploitative regime was better than no regime at all, or confusion as to what regime was operating. The results of this small-scale piece of research are shown in Appendix 8. The questionnaire used is Appendix 6. Ten specialist officers were asked to complete the questionnaire; 9 responded. No attempt was made to 'chase up' responses.

On Likert's scale overall the service's system of organisation seems to be somewhere between benevolent authoritative and consultative, perhaps slightly more System 3, consultative. However, there are a few points emerging from this that should be noted. Firstly there is a definite shift towards benevolent authoritative, from consultative in the area of decision-making and the extent to which subordinates feel they influence goals, methods and activity in the service, and more locally, their teams. Secondly there seems to be considerable confusion as to when and if we are operating System 2, benevolent authoritative, and System 3, consultative.

Lastly, there were a number of occasions when people recorded feeling they were in System 1 or System 4. Time could usefully be spent looking at communication systems operating in the organisation, attempting to be clearer regarding the difference between participation and consultation. This clarification may be particularly helpful for specialists who are often placed in a consultant role, or appear to be, without knowing when and where this role is appropriate. Sometimes misunderstandings occur when the consultant role is perceived by managers as undermining line management supervision.

In summary we have a bureaucratic organisation with personnel self-motivated to a large extent, not dependent on the 'carrot and stick' approach to work, and the organisation operating on consultative lines except perhaps for some decision-making processes. As this organisation has grown there has been a trend towards specialisation. The process of information-gathering and decision-making regarding the creation of a specialism is likely to be management collecting information about an area of work from a range of sources, including field staff, and then producing a plan for the creation of a specialism. Consultations regarding this plan are then likely to be undertaken. Comments made at the consultation stage would be noted by management who would then make the final decision. It would of course be hoped that the consultation process would create a commitment to the proposed specialism at fieldwork level but this can by no means be guaranteed. Wilkinson suggested in 1971 that managers have four options when faced with information that suggests change is necessary and that a decision needs to be taken. They can tell, sell, consult or involve. The manager that consults often creates a situation in which it is difficult to distinguish between consulting and involvement in decision-making.[10] Talented motivated staff will want to be involved in decision-making and will certainly not respond well to decisions that appear in conflict with their suggestions at the consultation stage. The manager will be faced with workers who are dissatisfied but find it hard to say why. This often leads to minor disagreements or a 'work to rule' attitude.

If this is true then some of the already created specialisms in the service may be struggling. Not because the decision was wrong but commitment to the task may be weak due to the process. This may cause problems when attempting to supervise a specialism. Is there clarity regarding objectives and expectations? Are we aware of all the implications regarding our expanding use of specialisms? Is there a commitment to the specialisms at all levels? To gain information on these aspects, sixteen specialists were interviewed. The line of questioning was open-ended. However, it was necessary to structure the interviews, and to do this an *aide memoire* was used (Appendix 7).

Given the openness of the questioning it was predictable there would be wide-ranging responses. These have been categorised and Tables 4.25—4.32 give some indications as to how those in specialist posts view their position.

Points which in my opinion are worthy of note from these Tables are:

(a)   Interviewees were able to talk a little about how they as individuals came into their present post but often had only a vague idea of how the post came into being and why (see Tables 4.25 and 4.29).

(b)   There seems to be a fairly wide range of reasons for specialisation to varying degrees in the service at present (see Table 4.25).

(c)   Few specialists have mild feelings about their work. It seems they quickly move to loving it or hating it (see Table 4.26).

(d)   Is the loss of autonomy within the service and increased managerial control a myth? The answers in Table 4.27 seem to suggest this. Those interviewed had wide-ranging feelings of accountability but managerial control did not seem all consuming (see Table 4.27).

Table 4.25 How did your specialism come about?

Number of times response mentioned	Type of response
6	A management initiative
6	Respond to a change in practice
4	A team initiative
4	Others
3	I've no idea
2	It's an amalgam of low priority tasks
2	Joint initiative between self and SPO
2	I was told it would help me get promotion

Table 4.26 How do you feel about your work?

Number of times response mentioned	Type of response
12	I'm enthusiastic
10	I'm depressed/miserable/angry/frustrated
8	It's challenging
7	I'm isolated
4	I feel confused and/or ignorant
3	It takes a long time to sort out role
2	Hope it will get me promotion

Table 4.27 To whom do you feel accountable?

Number of times response mentioned	Type of response
11	Recipients of the service (courts, clients)
6	Management
5	My own sense of professionalism
3	The community
3	Everybody (colleagues, public, clients, budget managers)
1	Nobody

Table 4.28 What support system exists?

Number of times response mentioned	Type of response
11	Little or none
8	Colleagues
3	Outside agencies
2	My SPO
2	The probation assistant
2	The management (HQ)
1	Clients

Table 4.29   On what basis are you specialising?

Number of times response mentioned	Type of response
9	I haven't a job specification
6	I have a specific task to perform
4	Don't know
4	We have identified a group of clients
3	I'm a permanent appointment
3	It's a team arrangement legitimised by management
3	It's a specialist method of working
2	It's an informal team arrangement
1	I have a gentleman's agreement

Table 4.30   What are your professional development and training needs?

Number of times response mentioned	Type of response
11	Basic training for my job
9	A support group
6	Advanced practice skills for my specialism
4	Better supervision from management
2	A skilled consultant re my specialism
2	Management skills
2	Don't know
2	Wider experience

Table 4.31   How or is your task to be evaluated?

Number of times response mentioned	Type of response
12	Erroneously talked about personal evaluations
7	No
3	Don't know
2	Yes — by courts and clients
2	Yes — team review carried out
1	My SPO did one via a reference
1	Through a staff meeting
1	Through on-going supervision

Table 4.32   How could your task be evaluated?

Number of times response mentioned	Type of response
11	Ask consumers what they think (court, clients)
5	Management and self should review
4	In-depth team reviews
4	Small-scale independent research
4	Use statistics and reports more often
1	Look at job specifications
1	Move away from personal evaluations

(e) The negative responses regarding support systems suggest cause for concern (see Table 4.28).

(f) Specialists do often seem vague about their task and the absence of job specifications sometimes increases this vagueness. Not everybody wants a written job specification but many would like an opportunity to clarify the boundaries of their task (see Table 4.29).

(g) When moving to a specialist post deficiency in training in certain areas is highlighted. Often the new task requires professional development and training opportunities to be provided (see Table 4.30).

(h) The question of sharing knowledge, experience and expertise via support groups seems worthy of consideration. It seems to make sense in terms of organisation, continuity and consistency, combating isolation and providing opportunities of learning from others, especially if county boundaries are crossed (see Table 4.30).

(i) The service finds it hard to even talk about task evaluations, we are so wrapped up in personal evaluations. There seems to be little task evaluation carried out, and what little there is often occurs as an afterthought or by accident (see Table 4.31).

(j) Perhaps we are a little precious about our activities, not wishing to ask consumers what they think of our product and rarely bringing in outside expertise (see Table 4.32).

Table 4.25 suggests that quite often specialisms drift into being with little thought taking place at organisation management level as to the long-term supervision of the development. The lack of comparison regarding workloads, the absence of information on trends concerning the specialism, how the specialist operates within the line management system, accountability, objectives and many other issues must all be considered carefully if problems are to be minimised in the future. Perhaps one of the biggest problems supervisors need to consider is the use made of expertise gained by specialists and the manner in which a specialist task is transferred from one member of staff to another. Interviewees commented on the lack of opportunity to work with the previous postholder of their specialism. This meant that valuable experience was wasted and the new incumbent duplicated mistakes made by the predecessor. Many interviewed felt they had some new skills to offer or share which the organisation was not using. The position was even more worrying when looking at one or two specialisms within teams. It is possible to observe a high level of expertise invested in one individual that would presumably be lost completely if the individual left the service.

Further problems emerge when the specialism has been operating for several years. How can the task be evaluated, how can projects be evaluated? (See Table 4.32) Statistics can be useful if the criteria for success have been quite clearly laid down at the beginning and a logical plan for collecting information is also drawn up. If this is not the case the success of a specialism or project can be portrayed a number of ways and will probably lead to stalemate. Of course times change and new criteria can be applied to a task with the intention of reviewing and perhaps improving its effectiveness but here a further difficulty emerges. Often by this time the specialist has a level of expertise superior to that of supervisors and will find it hard to understand if his/her views on what will or will not be successful are not accepted. Perhaps in this situation we could do worse than heed the suggestions of the specialists interviewed, particularly consulting consumers of the product and being more willing to consider small-scale independent research projects.

Clearly the development of specialisms in the service has been a complicated affair and suggestions for improving supervision should not be picked up without considerable thought regarding the overall picture. However, the following thoughts may be of value.

1   The service could try to avoid drifting into a specialism. If a case is made out it should be tested using available information and every effort should be made to clarify the objectives of the task. It may well be better to go for short-term objectives and regular reviews than long-term objectives that may well prove unattainable. Long-term objectives lead to vague supervision and the specialism or project can be measured as a failure any time in its life.

2   Job specifications may not always be appropriate, nor should they be treated as sacrosanct. However, the possibility of drawing up a job specification should always be at least considered as it does provide a framework for clarifying the task. Job specification with a length of time stipulated may be helpful. (See Table 4.29)

3   As a specialist develops expertise the support that can realistically be expected from line managers becomes questionable. However, specialists need to be clearly accountable to somebody in the organisation. Therefore it may be appropriate to separate professional development and support from accountability in these situations, thus making it easier for a line manager to ensure the task is being carried out whilst enabling the specialist opportunities for professional development and support in other forms. Perhaps support groups for specialists should be encouraged more, especially across county boundaries. (See Table 4.28)

4 We need to develop task evaluation and project evaluation skills within the organisation (see Tables 4.31 and 4.32).

5 If we wish to continue with a bureaucratic model for the organisation then line managers must learn to live with specialists. Line management rigidity will at best encourage duplication of effort and could in some cases prevent tasks from being carried out at all.

6 Avoid permanent appointments. Obviously people require job security but this need not be the same as security of the post. When developing new approaches or specialisms supervisors must ensure that staff in these areas feel safe to fail or conclude that the specialism has served its purpose. If we do not do this clearly, in some situations, encourage ineffective specialisms or projects. It must be made as easy as possible to acknowledge that a task or experiment has ended, and we must make it as easy as possible to dismantle these initiatives if appropriate. (See Tables 4.29 and 4.31)

Quotes from interviews

'If they don't know what to do they dump it on me.'
'Nobody bothers to see if I'm doing what I say I'm doing.'
'Wherever I went for support I became a supporter.'
'The other part of the county is a different world.'
'I'm frightened of getting out of touch.'
'We put our philosophy aside too much.'
'The ancillary gives me more support than anyone.'
'Nobody ever looked at effectiveness.'
'I've set up expectations. I should resign but I can't let them down.'
'I know about line management but it only hampers.'
'We're pretty self reliant.'
'It's a very personal specialism.'
'I suppose I'm a specialist in low priority tasks.'
'My line manager sympathises but he/she's too busy.'
'If this is a three year secondment do I justify special training?'

The recording of supervision

Supervision is a continuous process serving a variety of purposes. It is a complex affair, therefore it would seem sensible to have some sort of record which will aid the continuity and focus of the process. However, the apparent soundness of the idea does not mean that accurate recording of supervision is in reality desirable, achievable or commonplace. There are many difficulties. For example what would the status of a written record be? Is it simply an *aide memoire* between the parties involved or is it a more official document that could be used as evidence in a disciplinary matter? What should be recorded? Who should record and who should have access to the record? Unless issues like these are acknowledged and dealt with, recording supervision will fail to aid continuity and focus. Instead it will merely be an extra barrier to the frank and open atmosphere that supervisory processes need in order to be healthy.

The majority view of staff at all levels is that a record of supervision should be kept. All those interviewed for this research felt this and the research carried out by NAPO East Midlands branch in 1985 found this to be the case. The final East Midlands branch report states clearly that main grade staff feel 'Supervision is rarely recorded and individuals are often unable to differentiate between an expressed opinion and stated decision. Further, the evaluation process needs to be clarified and made explicit.'[11] The report continues:

Good supervision will be enhanced by open and shared recording. Such recording should not only detail length and frequency of supervision, but also allow for a shared contribution as to their content. The record will not only provide a working document in itself, but also allow for any instructions, assessments, disagreements and opinions to be made explicit, with all parties able to contribute. Joint and open recording will help to remove mutual suspicion and allow for a more open and honest relationship, enhancing the supporting and professional development aspects of supervision and providing a record which will also assist the agency in terms of monitoring and accountability.

It seems that the type of recording described above is felt by all staff to be the way things should be done. If this process was carefully adhered to we may reap the benefits described. Unfortunately for a variety of reasons the recording process is usually seen as an afterthought which brings the process into disrepute. It may well be significant that every assistant chief probation officer interviewed stated clearly that they kept a record of their supervision of seniors and that seniors were aware of this. Two representatives of this grade commented:

I've a book on each senior probation officer. They've all got access to it — it's county policy. But senior probation officers never ask to see it. I've also got personal files on everybody with a confusing array of information in them. I've been trying to think of a way to make sense of these.

I keep hand written notes — the senior probation officers are aware of this. These notes are used greatly for evaluations.

Seniors, however, were much more erratic in their recording of supervision. Not all think it advisable, some feel it can be appropriate with certain members of a team but not all members. Some feel they should be doing it but for a variety of reasons they don't. Even those who do record are not sure what the boundaries and objectives of the records should be. Here are three comments from seniors:

> I keep a record, yes. A book for each officer with notes. It's used as a basis for further discussions and used in evaluations. I've got one with negative comments on an officer with glowing evaluations written by my predecessor who didn't keep a record.

> I don't normally keep a record, it varies. Depends on the person. Take . . . he's insecure. He likes a record. He uses it. He quotes from it, uses it to back up his arguments. I normally rely on my memory.

> No I don't. The trouble with that system is you tend to only record the negatives and it's difficult to see people as a whole.

But what of field staff? Not one of the field officers interviewed knew if a record was kept of their supervision. Some had never given any thought to the matter. On thinking about it they felt there should be a record and they should be involved. Others had 'suspicions' but had never discussed the issue with their supervisors. A comment that summarised the general feeling ran as follows:

> I don't know if a record is kept. My last evaluation seemed to come off the top of his head. We didn't refer back to any supervision sessions. My new senior hasn't picked up much from my previous supervision or the evaluation.

The overall position seems messy which is unfortunate as staff at all grades feel there is much to be gained from good quality recording. Perhaps the reason for the messiness lies with the low priority this part of the supervisory task has been given. During several interviews people seemed to see it as a luxury they couldn't afford given other pressures. This may explain why recording supervision has hardly passed the 'good idea' stage. Recording supervision needs to be thought out and issues addressed at all levels. An interviewed assistant chief felt his notes from supervision were his property, an aid to his work with seniors, not to be used as official documents. Evaluations he said, were the official yardsticks. Thus he could record opinions, etc. However, another assistant chief felt recording was important as it 'could be used as evidence'. How can staff at any level be expected to confidently embark on recording of supervision if these issues are not discussed and resolved?

We must also clarify thinking and customise recording to meet individuals' service needs once a county policy has been reached. Several times in interview it became clear that supervisees had shown no interest in the recording of their supervision.

Such lack of interest is hardly likely to motivate a hard-pressed supervisor into improving practice in this area. Referral back to the East Midlands Working Party Report allows a glimpse of their members' attitudes to supervision. Eleven points are made under the heading *Members attitude to supervision* which are summarised as follows:

1   Supervision mainly consists of the traditional one-to-one counselling approach which many staff are dissatisfied with.
2   Supervision is normally initiated by senior probation officers who set the agendas.
3   Supervision is rarely recorded.
4   Supervision tends to reflect the needs of management.
5   The emphasis on confidentiality is problematical.
6   Supervision is affected by the nature of the relationship between the parties.
7   Frequency and quality of supervision deteriorates as probation officers become more experienced.
8   There is no clear thread to supervision.
9   Evaluation can lead to mistrust, bitterness and a poor relationship between supervisor/supervisee.
10   Speed of change in the service can be problematical.
11   Supervision often leads to dead ends as opportunities to act on acknowledged problems often do not arise.

A well recorded supervisory process could play a significant part in improving most if not all of the issues raised by these eleven points. The task of recording is as vital as that. Finding a procedure which is of value to all grades requires an effort from all levels in the service. It is not likely that a national set of guidelines in the recording of supervision would be helpful regardless of its origin — ACOP, NAPO, HO, etc. The reality is that individual services have different policies, priorities, personnel and problems. Individual services looking for a consensus view as to their service's supervisory needs would seem more likely to reap the benefits that are clearly available for those who take the recording of supervision seriously.

Informal supervision

Without fail, any discussion regarding staff supervision in the probation service will include references to 'informal supervision' and its merits or otherwise. The focus of the questionnaires sent out was formal supervision, although there were opportunities for respondents to refer to informal supervision and many people did. During subsequent interviews the question of informal supervision was often discussed at length, particularly its boundaries and quality.

There is complete agreement within the service that informal supervision in the widest sense of the phrase is a valuable component of the supervisory process. The term was used during this research to cover a wide range of situations including staff-room conversations, exchanging thoughts in a car, crisis consultations, discussion groups. Even discussions about personal problems or attitudes to life were seen by some as part of the informal supervision process. However, the agreement is based on an assumption that the informal process is a supplement to an agreed formal process. Where this is the case all concerned agree the foundations have been laid for an acceptable supervisory process. Many senior probation officers made the point, when returning questionnaires, that they had answered the questions regarding formal supervision but that this had only partially covered the supervisory task. There were many similar comments, such as 'I also operate an open door policy'. But if we agree that this creature known as informal supervision is so vital to the process, what is it? What are its objectives and limitations? How do I know if I'm involved in an informal supervisory session? Is anything ever 'off the record'? What does the phrase 'open door policy' mean?

Assistant chief officer comments suggest that they feel managers need to be able to respond quickly to crisis situations. However they acknowledge, as do senior probation officers, that in reality there is no such thing as an 'open door policy' in the sense that managers are always available. What they mean is: 'Come in when you like if I'm not busy doing something else'. As they are often busy the open door policy becomes a frustrating game of heads popping around doors and apologising for the interruption! The feelings of many in this grade can perhaps be summarised by the following comment from an assistant chief. Seniors, he said, should be 'available on a consultancy basis'. When pressed to amplify this it was made clear that he was not advocating a return to casework consultancy. It was more about advising on county policy, resource availability and legitimising staff decisions in difficult situations.

Field staff recognise the value of informal opportunities to explore issues and problems in their work. Interestingly they seem much happier with the notion of informality when talking about sharing with colleagues, or senior managers other than their immediate line manager. Informal supervision from your immediate superior is viewed with some anxiety. For example: 'Present senior will see any member of his team on request. I do not think this is the best way to go about things.' This was said by an officer not receiving any formal supervision but even those receiving a blend of formal and informal are anxious about the latter with an immediate supervisor. Yet again much will depend on the quality of relationships within the team and the supervisor's credibility.

Several investigations into the meaning of informal supervision as perceived by field staff led the author to conclude that it was not uncommon for it to develop amongst colleagues as a response to a feeling that the line manager was not helpful to team members. Occasionally it was a response to the complete absence of supervision from the line manager:

> Supervision has only a negligible effect on my working life. I give little and I receive little — it's a game we all play. By and large I tend to look to my team for what I feel I need, for 'supervision' on an informal basis.

Eight officers (9.1 per cent) appeared to be receiving no formal supervision but there was an informal arrangement of some kind. It could be argued that at least they were better off than the remainder of the 18.6 per cent of field staff who do not receive any form of supervision at all, but even so they are clearly not happy with the informal or 'open door' policy. Of the eight, six were critical and two were non-committal.

The informal process can clearly be a useful component of supervision. It can, unfortunately, be used to disguise bad supervisory practice. Several times the author observed the informal supervision model being used collusively by a supervisor and supervisee to avoid contact with each other.

Informality = nothing (a tragedy or farce written for the probation service)

Scene 1   Basic philosophical and/or political and/or personality conflicts between supervisees and supervisor.

Scene 2   The unresolved conflicts lead to mutual suspicion that in turn produces unproductive and unpleasant line management supervision.

Scene 3   All concerned unhappy with the situation, review the supervisory process as this is easier than bringing the basic conflicts into the open.

Scene 4   Conflict reduced by removing the supervisor from the firing line via the introduction of an informal process allowing

Scene 5   supervisees to determine the level of conflict engaged in. By way of thanks supervisees periodically bring non-issues to the supervisor who is able to 'help'. Supervisor thanks supervisees by ignoring areas of conflict and lets them get on with it.

'If you do not get on particularly well with the senior you don't push to see him/her more often' — a probation officer.

This scenario demonstrates how easy it is to abuse the notion of informal supervision. How can we reduce that danger? Perhaps the first step should be to assess what the informal aspect can and cannot deal with.

Formal pre-arranged supervision suggests a considered continuous process which can allow themes to develop. The very nature of informality is likely to prevent such development. It will not be a continuous process therefore it seems likely that the informal sessions can only be helpful if each time they have a clear task and that at the end of the session decisions can be taken that allow the worker to move on with that task. It is in essence a consultation process which Kadushin describes as one in which 'Clearly defined, clearly circumscribed and delimited problems which can be dealt with in a limited period of time'.[12]

If used in this way then the informal process is extremely helpful but this also gives us clear indications as to those areas that should not be dealt with on this basis. For example many seniors mentioned the use made of supervisory sessions when preparing personal evaluations. Much is made of the supervision and evaluation process as a form of continuous assessment. If this is so it suggests that issues that may arise in an evaluation should not be dealt with on an informal basis. If it is continuous assessment those involved need regular opportunities to review progress in any area that gives cause for concern. Furthermore the informal process is notoriously hard to record. Indeed the question needs to be asked should informal supervision be recorded? If it is and is then used in an evaluation is it legitimate to still call it informal? Would this kind of supervision not be better described as disorganised supervision? Other areas that could be described as professional development issues would appear to be unsuitable for informal supervision. Identifying training and development needs requires those involved to look at patterns and trends in working practice. Lastly, perhaps obviously, issues concerning basic competence or disciplinary matters should not be dealt with in this way. Of course in many situations supervisors will feel that a 'quiet word' is the best way to deal with a minor problem.

110

This is probably correct but the supervisee needs to know how important the message is, and this is often difficult in an informal situation. Supervisees should not be left thinking 'Did he/she mean that?'.

If it is correct that the informal process without formal pre-arranged supervision cannot deal with developmental issues those teams operating this way have a recipe for long-term problems. In the short term those involved will feel they are getting support on day-to-day issues. However, absence of longer-term review, the acknowledgement of working patterns and trends, feedback on performance, the identifying of professional development needs will lead those involved into a 'dead end'. This is not to say that formal supervision must always be carried out by the line manager, but it is management responsibility to ensure a process is available that will allow all staff to share and review their professional development. 'Staff do need to reflect on their work but not necessarily with their managers. However the manager must ensure the option to reflect is available.'[13]

When looking to the supervision seniors receive it is surprising that informal supervision was not mentioned more often as many claim not to be receiving much via the formal process. Only one senior commented on the informal links with his line manager saying that 'We chat and support each other'.

There was little evidence that seniors or assistant chiefs use their colleagues for informal supervision although several talked about 'little chats'. However, when pressed to comment on the value of these, those that mentioned them did not give them much credibility, commenting more on the dangers of getting dragged into gossip than their value as a constructive process.

Notes

1   NAPO East Midlands Branch Working Party Report on Supervision, 1984.
2   Ibid.
3   Payne and Scott, *Developing Supervision of Teams in Field and Residential Social Work, Part 1*, National Institute for Social Work, Paper no. 12, 1982.
4   East Midlands Probation Services, *Staff Supervision: Care and Control?*, NAPO, 1986.
5   Ibid.
6   Home Office Circular 113/77, *Probation and After-Care Service, Ethnic Minorities*, 1977.

7   Booth, Martin and Melotte, *Specialisation: Issues in the Organisation of Social Work*, chapter 7, BASW publication, 1980.
8   Weber, M., *The Theory of Social and Economic Organisation*, 1964.
9   McGregor, D., *The Human Side of Enterprise*.
10   Wilkinson, A., *Information for Managers*, chapter 11, Pitmans Publishing Company, 1971.
11   East Midlands Probation Services, *Staff Supervision: Care and Control?*, NAPO, 1986.
12   Kadushin, A., *Consultations in Social Work*, Columbia University Press, 1977.
13   East Midlands Probation Services, *Staff Supervision: Care and Control?*, NAPO, 1986.

5 Supervision models

It is encouraging to find agreement on so many aspects of staff supervision across all grades. It is clear that the whole service is united in thinking that:

(a) Supervision is essential.
(b) The component parts of supervision must include ensuring minimum standards are adhered to, support and professional development.
(c) Good supervision is likely to be a blend of informal and formal arrangements, but that a formally agreed system must be provided, endorsed by management at all levels.
(d) Supervisory models must reflect the uniqueness of services, area teams and individuals within a team.
(e) Speed of change within the service requires regular reviews of the supervisory processes.
(f) There is room for improvement.

Given this situation there may be many in the service who recognise the value of improving the process but find the task of initiating change a daunting one. This chapter reviews the efforts of a number of services and individuals to up-date supervisory processes and make them more relevant to service need. A number of supervisory models has emerged in recent years and a few of these are summarised. Whilst each of the models has emerged during the author's research and the work of a number of people has been quoted, it has been necessary to adapt the models in order that they relate to probation practice in a reasonably concise manner. It is accepted that each supervisory process should be unique, there is no right or wrong model.

Model one — the continuous review

The first problem any individual or group of people wishing to improve their supervisory process is likely to face is simply how to undertake a review of the current process. Payne and Scott[1] suggest the stages should be as follows:

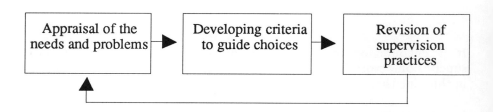

Figure 5.1

As Figure 5.1 suggests Payne and Scott see the process as continuous, acknowledging the development of the service and the individuals working in it. They also helpfully provide examples of this process operating within a social service department. If this process were transferred to a fictitious probation field team it might look something like the process suggested below.

Example

A probation field team   The team consists of 7 probation officers, 2 probation assistants, 4 clerical staff and a senior probation officer. The team is based in the middle of the 'patch'. It has responsibility for all types of cases arising in its area, including civil work and community service. One officer specialises in the former, another officer and an assistant specialise in the latter. One officer is in his first year as is one assistant. The rest are all experienced (i.e. over three years in post) including one officer nearing retirement.

Task 1 — assess current supervision practice The current practice is mainly individual sessions with the senior. However, due to the size of the team and workload pressures these sessions are not as frequent, lengthy or planned as all those involved would like them to be. However, there is a considerable amount of 'informal supervision' as the senior probation officer tries to operate an open door policy and team members try to be mutually supportive.

Primarily team members go their own way with case loads, supervising in the style they feel comfortable with. There is a limited amount of joint work. There have been attempts at group work but referrals into groups have historically been patchy. The team have talked about the need for some kind of day-care facility as 80 per cent of caseloads are unemployed. Agreement has not been reached on how to go about this.

The senior is accountable for the team's work to an assistant chief who also has a 'patch'.

Task 2 — assess current team needs Most members of the team want to be more adventurous and creative but this must be within existing resources. However, this is only formally expressed in the fortnightly team meetings. Apart from these meetings there is little opportunity to pool ideas and develop strategies. The specialists could easily be marginalised if the team develops. Attempts to use the team meetings as a developmental forum are regularly frustrated by the amount of day-to-day business that the meeting has to deal with.

Isolation needs to be reduced. More interchanging of tasks could well be beneficial (e.g. could the two probation service assistants merge their respective tasks and be more mutually supportive?). Individuals need to be encouraged to share more. Consider ways of joint working. Caseload similarities. Be more aware of skills within the group.

Task 3 — assess individual team members' needs The needs of the individuals are related to supervision objectives and their individual career development, and to the team's needs for its next stage of development.

1 All staff need to be able to improve their contribution to team development. They also need to share and use the different skills in the group.

115

2 The first year officer needs to understand agency objectives, priorities, policies and working practices. It is also important he knows more about needs and resources in the area, and to plan work as a full caseload develops.

3 The new assistant needs to understand the philosophy of the service and be clear about professional boundaries and nature of task.

4 The civil work specialist needs support, training re specialism and to remain part of the team.

5 The community service officer and assistant need to remain part of the group and communications between field and community service workers need to be improved. The community service assistant is hoping to obtain a place on a CQSW course next year and wants professional development opportunities.

6 The experienced staff are committed and talented. They need a positive response to their desire to be more adventurous. They need professional challenges.

7 The officer nearing retirement is still very active but practice is out of date. He has worked in the area for years and is well known by everybody including local magistrates who think he is a fine example of the good old days when they knew what probation stood for!

8 The clerical staff need better understanding of the task and practice of the service, particularly as they rotate reception and telephone duties.

9 All staff could benefit from improved group work and activity planning skills.

10 One experienced officer needs to improve her administration work, particularly case recording.

11 The senior probation officer needs to develop understanding of team needs and develop supervisory skills that enable him to offer worthwhile supervision to all staff. This is not to be confused with personally supervising all staff.

Evaluating current practice   Current supervision is seen as adequate but needs development. Most team members realise this but have no coherent basis for extending the search for alternatives. The current practice supports and monitors the work of individuals but cannot cope with promoting and supporting a change in team identity and in supporting more joint working by team members. The present scheme is too dependent on the senior probation officer.

Developing the supervision scheme   Taking into account current strengths, supervision practice and aspirations, the following might be developed:

1 *The regular team meetings will be weekly* with the following features:
   Strictly time limited to 1½ hours.
   Pre-circulated agenda from chair person.
   Rotating chair using all team members.
   A representative of clerical staff to attend team meetings.
   The meetings will concentrate on team policies and strategies.
   The chair may use team leader as consultant when putting agenda together and when chairing meeting.

2 *The experienced officers will meet monthly for case discussions.* Chair to rotate. Chair responsible for obtaining two cases for discussion each month.

3 *Civil worker to join a group of civil work specialists beyond patch boundaries as a support group.* However continues to attend team meetings and will have a bi-monthly slot in team meetings to share practice issues with colleagues.

4 *Community service workers also join support group outside patch boundary* and have bi-monthly slot in team meetings.

5 *First year officers to have weekly supervision sessions with the senior probation officer,* as well as attending team meetings.

6 *Officer nearing retirement to meet with senior probation officer fortnightly for next six months to plan for retirement* in terms of his clients, general workload and the creation of space and opportunity to work through anxieties about this.

7 *Two topic groups to be convened.* Team to agree on topics which give cause for concern re current service delivery. Objective — to see if service could be improved. (Day-care likely to be one of first topics looked at.)

8 *Team to agree on an evaluation procedure and timetable* for the coming year which meets agency requirements.

9 *Senior probation officer to randomly select ten case records each month for inspection.* Feedback on the randomly selected cases to be given to officers individually. Include positive as well as negative feedback where appropriate.

10 *Senior probation officer to inform management* of proposed supervisory developments and negotiate the endorsement of these arrangements.

11 *Senior probation officer to consider implications* of team proposals on resources and workloads. Engage senior management in discussion regarding team aspirations and resource implications.

12 *Senior probation officer to arrange team 'away day' in six*
    months' time to review progress and allow team to make suitable
    amendments in the light of developments.
13 *Senior probation officer and an experienced officer (possibly our*
    friend nearing retirement) to organise quarterly information
    sessions for clerical staff. Half-day sessions on aspects of pro-
    bation work aimed at familiarising clerical staff with service task
    and practice.
14 *Senior probation officer to discuss with training officer training*
    needs of team and look for appropriate training events.

This hypothetical example demonstrates that when the supervisory
processes are reviewed a blend of supervisory styles is likely to emerge.
The key lies with regular reviews of the process. This brings
supervision to life and avoids the trap of merely inspecting and
monitoring which leads to apathy or worse, hostility.

Model two — blended supervision (functional and patch)

A review of supervisory processes is likely to highlight the need to
review management style before the details of supervision can be
addressed. Should management operate on a geographical patch
basis or on a functional basis? Should management have general
supervisors or break down the components of supervision thus allowing the development of inspectors, managers, developers and
consultants. Individual services will wish to organise themselves
in different ways but once again the key is likely to be regular
reviews. A service management operating on a patch basis in the
1970s may well find a switch to functional management beneficial
in the 1980s. Blending the two is also quite possible but requires
considerable planning and is likely to take two or three years for
all staff to adjust. The blending of functional and patch responsibilities is currently being tried in several services at present. The
model described here is a composite of several blends observed by
the author.

Figure 5.2 illustrates the arrangements made at chief officer level.
It can be seen that each of the three assistant chiefs has a combination of patch and functional responsibilities. The functions may
be a certain aspect of the task (e.g. prisons) or a stressful area of
professional practice (e.g. non-accidental injury matters). It can
also be seen that each assistant chief has a group of senior probation
officers and responsibilities blending function and patch. With such
a high degree of overlap it becomes vital that the chief probation

118

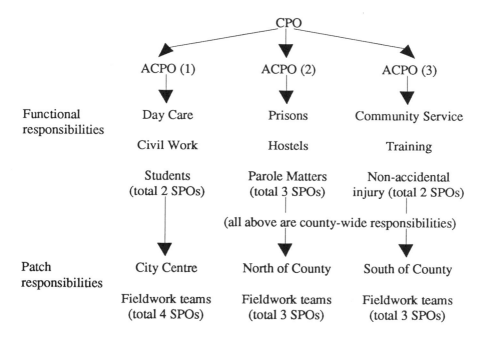

CPO

ACPO (1)   ACPO (2)   ACPO (3)

Functional   Day Care   Prisons   Community Service
responsibilities

                    Civil Work   Hostels   Training

                    Students   Parole Matters   Non-accidental
                    (total 2 SPOs)   (total 3 SPOs)   injury (total 2 SPOs)

                              (all above are county-wide responsibilities)

Patch   City Centre   North of County   South of County
responsibilities

                    Fieldwork teams   Fieldwork teams   Fieldwork teams
                    (total 4 SPOs)   (total 3 SPOs)   (total 3 SPOs)

Figure 5.2

officer brings his assistant chief probation officers together frequently to discuss developments, offer mutual support and to develop an atmosphere that encourages a frank exchange of views and constructive criticism. The supervision system offered to assistant chiefs therefore is likely to be based on the notion of senior management team supervision.

If we pursue the supervisory process down the line management system we see further blending reflecting the functional/patch approach. Figure 5.3 illustrates the arrangements made by the assistant chief probation officer (1) for supervising his/her responsibilities. We can see from Figure 5.3 that the assistant chief has taken his/her patch responsibilities and arranged them into a blend of functional and patch. In this situation it may well be that the supervisory model will need to reflect the varying degrees of overlap.

119

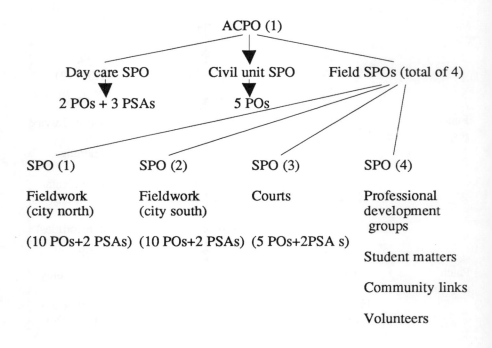

Figure 5.3

To supervise each of the six SPOs as individuals with occasional group meetings would probably not be an adequate system to meet the group's needs. For example, a good case could be made for supervising the two fieldwork SPOs together as consistency of practice is vital. However, the civil work SPO may well value individualised sessions and may not need to be heavily involved with the rest of the group, acknowledging of course the dangers of being isolated. The linking-up of the various tasks may well be the most important role for the assistant chief probation officer in this situation, therefore city centre service delivery meetings may well be beneficial, the focus being on the quality of linking between SPOs. Supervision may be based on the notion of sub-groups or pairs focused on service delivery with full-group meetings being used to share information. Individual supervision could be personally negotiated with periodic reviews of individual needs built in. Quality of service within such a group may well depend largely on the quality of teamwork achieved. Therefore a good case could be made for senior probation officer group involvement in task appraisal reports. Groups such as this need to 'own' the level of co-operation and support they provide.

Moving down the line to teams, blending can still be pursued. Figure 5.4 illustrates the arrangements of a fieldwork senior probation officer.

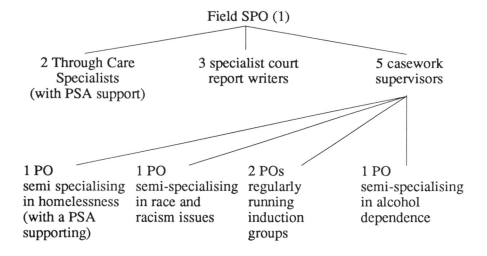

Figure 5.4

Although there is a high degree of functional working in this group there are still traces of patch working. For example, the through-care workers have divided prisons in the catchment area between them to maximise efficiency in prison visiting. The officers developing expertise in homelessness and racism issues try to pick up cases in those patches in the city where these concerns are vital. The senior must evolve a range of supervisory styles to cope with the demands of such a team. Firstly the career stages of individuals must be recognised. Obviously new officers need regular and frequent supervision from the line manager, more experienced staff may not need frequent meetings. Following a review of supervisory needs the team decides on the following format:

1 Any first year officer or assistant has weekly supervision from their SPO during their first year.
2 Other staff receive senior probation officer supervision based on agreed need.
3 There will be a weekly allocation and information sharing meeting.
4 The three sub-groups (through-care, social enquiry reports and casework) will each meet monthly with senior probation officer to develop professional practice.
5 The senior probation officer will take a random sample of work monthly in order to monitor quality of work. Issues arising from this will be taken up with individuals. However, if a pattern emerges the senior probation officer will place the issue on the information-sharing meeting agenda.
6 There will be two 'away days' each year which will look at the quality of service delivery and team support systems.
7 Roles within the team will be reviewed annually. No team member should stay in the same area of work more than three years.

This is a hypothetical arrangement, no service visited by the author had such a system although several had elements of it. Such systems demonstrate admirable flexibility and therefore can respond to changing needs. The difficulty is that they often, as the example shows, need a complicated communication system which means there must be a strong commitment to the method from all concerned.

Model three — the 'risk' or 'dangerousness' model

Some supervisory models are based on an assessment of risk or dangerousness within service workload. High risk or dangerous cases are seen as requiring more intensive supervision than run of the mill cases. Such systems require officers to prioritise their caseload and regularly review these priorities. At first sight this type of supervision may seem to place great emphasis on inspection and accountability whilst offering little support. However, its advantage is that in high risk cases in which the worker often feels very exposed, the system re-quires line managers to take part in case planning and be accountable for decisions taken concerning the case.

Table 5.1 is the simplest form of this method. As can be seen, it does not include consultations with teams, other agencies, etc. These can be built into a system if a service so desires. However, it must be remembered that cases can be moving in and out of the priority categories quickly, therefore a cumbersome system may collapse.

Table 5.1

Type of case		Type of supervision
Low priority cases	—	Random checks by senior probation officer.
	—	Subject of case discussion if probation officer or senior probation officer request this.
Medium risk cases	—	Random checks by senior probation officer.
	—	Quarterly discussion with senior probation officer, re progress and future strategy.
	—	Subject of case discussion if probation officer or senior probation officer request this.
High risk cases	—	Once identified by probation officer and senior probation officer, assistant chief probation officer notified details of case.
	—	Assistant chief probation officer then requests quarterly updates of case.
	—	When received, assistant chief probation officer either signs approval or arranges tripartite meeting re case.
	—	Senior probation officer and probation officer must discuss case quarterly and agree future strategy.
	—	Tripartite case discussion can be convened at any time by any one of the three people involved.

Model four — decentralised supervision

Decentralised in this context means separating the various components of supervision and giving them to different people. The idea stems from the East Midlands Conference entitled 'Care and Control'.[2] During one of the small group sessions this model was suggested. However, the idea was not fully developed during that conference due to lack of time. The author has attempted to put the idea into a workable form.

The model stems from an acknowledgement that staff supervision in probation has a number of essential but not entirely compatible components. Elements identified in supervision include:

(a) Accountability
(b) Support
(c) An opportunity to reflect on work performance
(d) Future planning to meet team objectives.

It was felt that seniors attempting to meet all these needs using the traditional one-to-one method of staff supervision together with (hopefully) regular team meetings were unlikely to produce a genuinely effective model. Decentralised supervision could be an alternative, although it must be acknowledged this is only a crude outline and any team adopting this model would need to refine and customise it to meet their own individual team needs.

Accountability

It is accepted that the service needs to ensure that stated standards of work are adhered to. It is also accepted that individual members of staff are accountable through the line management system to the service regarding their work. However, vital though the monitoring of standards and a clear system of accountability are, they can hinder other aspects of supervision, such as the offering of support and of opportunities to honestly reflect on work performance. It was therefore suggested that accountability should be more clearly separated from the other aspects of supervision and more clearly and thoroughly catered for. This could be achieved by team seniors undertaking a quarterly accountability check on the team's current workload, the objectives of these quarterly checks being spelt out and the procedure for dealing with resulting anxieties being agreed within the team. Carrying out the quarterly checks and dealing with issues arising from them would clearly be the task of the senior.

Support

Support systems can and will vary enormously, but it would be helpful if more thought could be given to their development across teams and that these systems should have agreed terms of reference and be validated by management. With service tasks ever widening and more officers developing special interests or having a degree of specialist tasks to carry out, small support groups of those with similar special interests or tasks could be extremely helpful.

Performance reflection

It is felt that the opportunity to reflect on work performance in a safe environment is essential to all staff at all levels. However, the service evaluation process, focusing as it often does largely on individuals rather than job appraisal and carrying with it judgements which affect career prospects, make the waters very murky for seniors who try to offer their staff this facility. It was suggested that this aspect of supervision could be dealt with rather better by allowing team members to split into sub-groups. Once again the implications of this procedure would need to be looked at carefully by individual teams, boundaries agreed and validated by management, but it may well offer team members a much needed opportunity to 'officially' unburden themselves and share stress in a safe environment.

Future planning

Planning for the future to meet agreed team objectives suggests that the focal point for this element of supervision should be the team itself. Seniors are now expected to annually review team objectives and agree them with management based on the Statement of Local Objectives and Priorities. Teams should, and it is felt would, accept responsibility for working on these objectives and trying to achieve them. Clearly in striving to meet them teams may highlight resource or training needs which require management attention. The role of the senior in this area thus becomes vitally important as co-ordinator and facilitator of team needs.

It is also important to say that whilst this model separates staff supervision into four clear components there will clearly be overlaps and not only would any team considering the model need to refine it to meet its own needs, but would also need to agree a good deal of flexibility in trying to operate it, particularly in the first year. Anybody considering such a model would need to build in regular team and management reviews of the process.

Model five — staff focused supervision

It is to be hoped that any supervisory model would have as one of its primary objectives the needs of individual members of staff. However, individual needs are not always the starting point as the other models in this chapter reveal. Payne and Scott[3] suggest a range of supervisory styles which require the supervisor to look closely at the needs of individual staff if they are to play a full part in meeting the agency task. They refer to 'arrangements' by which they mean the configuration of people who interact around supervision tasks. Styles may range from one-to-one professional development counselling through to a full-blooded team approach in which the supervisor operates as an equal member of the group.

We can see from Figure 5.5 that any number of these styles could be operating within a team at one time and the manager's role as co-ordinator and facilitator of these styles could well be more important than their supervisory role in an experienced talented team. However, Payne and Scott do add a note of caution which has been strongly

ARRANGEMENT		FEATURE	WHO IS INVOLVED			EXTERNAL CONSULTANT
			WORKERS	SUPERVISOR		
Individual or Tutorial	(1)	The team or unit leader supervises an individual worker, formally and privately. This may be backed up by informal modelling on the job.	Individual		Yes	Unlikely
Pair	(2)	The team leader supervises two staff together. Both formal direct supervision and modelling on the job are likely. Often used for new or inexperienced staff.	Two similar workers		Yes	Unlikely
Tandem	(3)	Two team members supervise each other. Each remains responsible for their own decisions. Suitable for two equally experienced workers.	Two similar experienced workers		No, only as monitor	Possible
Tag	(4)	One worker is attached as a shadow to an experienced worker to learn from observation.			Yes	Unlikely
Supervision Group	(5)	A group of staff with identical needs and/or resources works together on a limited agenda related to those needs. The role is not dissimilar from that carried in individual tutorial arrangements.		Yes		Possible
Peer groups	(6)	As above, but where the group members share the responsibility for the work more easily identified as belonging to one individual. May well be a natural development of the supervision group, the team leader having facilitated this.			No, only to monitor	Possible
Team Supervision	(7)	Differs from 5 & 6 above in that all team members are included regardless of disparity of the needs or resources of individuals. It is essentially focused on the work of the team itself rather than working with individuals in the context of a group of peers.		Yes		Possible

Figure 5.5   Summary of supervision arrangements

reinforced by those involved in this research. Care must be taken to avoid the 'lump' approach. Without wishing to discourage development we must be sure that the notion of group supervision is not embraced as a way of throwing a multitude of problems and issues into one large pot and hoping somehow that 'the group' will sort it out. Payne and Scott encourage 'the selective development of group approaches'. They also advocate the use of nominal group technique in group supervision. Brainstorming in groups has been popular for many years, but it has a number of limitations. In many group situations the nominal group technique will get a more positive response.

Nominal group technique — practical stages

1   The group assembles to work on a common task. This task is often represented by a sentence completion, for example, 'One way of dealing with violence in the hostel could be . . . '.
2   Each member of the group works alone silently and privately, but sitting within the confines of the group, a time limit will be used. Those who complete the task earlier remain silent, thus nobody who needs all the time is disadvantaged.
3   Each group member reads out aloud what they have written and this is recorded on a flip board.
4   At the end of this phase several options may be selected. For example questions of clarification may be asked, systematic analysis of commonalities or differences may be undertaken, or perhaps a free flowing discussion may be encouraged. Sometimes some form of agenda building or priority selection may be done.

By adopting this technique when considering important issues it blends in a unique way a number of important group work features. It carries the encouragement of individual responsibility to work on a group task and the collective effort, with individual vivacity or personal dominance restricted. It creates a culture whereby each individual has both rights and obligations to be heard and it mirrors the themes of team work. For those reasons it seems to be a useful system to adopt in group supervision.[4]

Model six — differential supervision

Differential supervision is the name used by Kenneth Watson to describe a range of supervisory models devised by the Chicago childcare society in the early 1970s.[5] In many respects Watson's models were similar to those of Payne and Scott but the range of models evolved from an assessment of supervision objectives with individuals rather than a team review. Watson's models place considerable emphasis on the different roles a supervisor may have depending on the individual being supervised. His starting-point was to divide the various tasks of supervision into two categories — teaching and administrative functions. Watson suggests that when a supervisee's needs are gathered under these two headings the type of supervision required is likely to emerge. Therefore it is important to have a range of models available. The six types evolved by the Chicago child-care society are described below:

(a) *Tutorial model*   A one-to-one relationship in which the supervisor can teach the supervisee. Useful for inexperienced staff or for experienced staff at the request of the supervisee.

(b) *Case consultation*   A one-to-one meeting with a designated consultant with the supervisee scheduling the contacts as needed and setting the agenda.

(c) *The supervisory group*   A supervisor operating with a group of supervisees, a form of group tutorial. Supervisees would probably need to be at a similar stage of development. If the group is too diverse it becomes hard to find a meaningful focus for learning.

(d) *Peer group supervision*   No designated supervisor, a group of equals. The group should be able to share skills and experiences. Needs a chairperson, meets regularly with equal access to the agenda. Individuals still responsible for their own decisions regarding their professional practice, the group only has advisory powers. Accountability issues would have to be dealt with through traditional line management procedures.

(e) *Tandem supervision*   A pairing of workers who learn about each other's workload and develop a collaborative approach to their tasks. As with the peer group model accountability is dealt with via line management but the pair offers consulting and support facilities.

(f) *Team supervision*   A full blooded team approach to supervision requires regular meetings, good planning and agenda setting and chairmanship. This is a decision-making group and individuals are bound by corporate responsibility. However, the team must know the boundaries the agency has set for its decision-making powers and still needs to be able to hold the team accountable for carrying out its task. Therefore accountability divided. The team leader ensures individuals are carrying out the task and the agency-set minimum standards which must be adhered to.

A further development of the roles of supervision has been provided by Yona Cohen. Like Watson he identified the need for supervisors to provide consultancy and teaching facilities. However, he also highlighted the need for supervisors to be prepared to undertake other roles such as supporter, judge, representative of the agency and bureaucrat.

The supporter role is essentially an acknowledgement of the stressful nature of probation work and the conflicting demands that sometimes emerge.

> Probation officers operate under emotional stress which when 'sufficiently' accumulated, is expressed by cynicism, fatalism and by dysfunction and emotional defences. Such development may in itself reduce the chances of effective intervention. The probation officer's optimism is in itself a factor conducive to success. Help and verbal support offered by the supervisor to the probation officer to conduct their work in an atmosphere of confidence promotes a positive outcome.[6]

The judge role as described by Cohen concerns the delicate balance between befriending and controlling. Cohen suggests that the probation service supervisors should constantly keep this in mind and let the officer know if they feel the balance is wrong. It is once again an acknowledgement that there are strong pressures on field staff, and a committed officer wanting to help clients will often need a supervisor to assess whether a functional distance is being kept.

The role of agency representatives concerns the crucial task of the middle manager within the organisation's communication system. It is an acknowledgement that 'Lines of communication in a hierarchy tend to be partially selective in transmitting context. There is a quantitative difference between input and output and changes occur in the content, in emphasis and in tone.'[7] The middle manager can easily over identify with senior management or field workers. Keeping an in-between position is vital but very difficult. Failure to do this is likely to lead to serious disagreements between senior management and field workers in the long term.

The role of bureaucrat stems from an acknowledgement that his/her authority comes from his/her position in the hierarchy. This requires the supervisor to relate to team members in a neutral way. This is often difficult as the supervisor may have a 'professional' view that they would like to voice. However, on occasions the bureaucrat role requires the professional voice to remain silent. Of course the supervisor who operates purely in the bureaucrat mode, never demonstrating a capacity for professional support or integrity, will quickly run into another set of problems.

Cohen's set of roles is in tune with the work of Tibbert in the 1960s.[8] She saw supervision as:

(a) Support
(b) Education
(c) Context.

She also felt that supervisees should be seen in three distinct ways:

1. The worker as a person
2. The worker as a professional
3. The worker as an employee.

Thus a probation officer suffering a bereavement in his/her family would need the supervisory emphasis placed on support whilst the dominant factor in the way the supervisor saw the team member would be 'the worker as a person'.

The works of Watson, Cohen and Tibbert all suggest that the supervisor be aware and skilled in a number of roles and that a review of supervisory needs should demonstrate the need for a particular role to be adopted.

Model seven — action centred leadership

In recent years the action centred model has been put forward by both the South West and Midlands regional training development units as a useful model for newly promoted senior probation officers to consider. It is based on the work of John Adair[9] and provides new seniors with three clear elements to work on in terms of developing practice, together with an outline of the team leader view and a useful checklist to which new seniors can refer, to ensure they are carrying out their contribution to the team's task effectively. Figure 5.6 shows the elements that Adair suggests cover the key areas of need — achieving the task, building the team and developing the individual.

It can be seen that the key areas overlap and failure in any one of the three will substantially hamper progress in the other two. Therefore the team leader needs to be clear about the contribution they should make in each of the three areas if the team is to be successful. The South West and Midlands regional staff development units offer the following helpful lists for newly appointed seniors:

Figure 5.6

Achieving the task

The leader's main contribution to achieving the required result lies in:

(a) Being quite clear what the task is;
(b) Understanding how it fits into the overall short- and long-term objectives of the organisation;
(c) Planning how he will accomplish it;
(d) Defining and providing the resources needed, including the time and the authority required;
(e) Doing all possible to ensure that the organisational structure allows the task to be done effectively;
(f) Controlling progress towards the goal;
(g) Evaluating results and comparing them with the goals and the plans.

Developing individuals

If the needs of the individual are to be satisfied at work they:

(a) Must feel a sense of personal achievement in the job they are doing, that they are making a worthwhile contribution to the objectives of the group or section;
(b) Must feel that the job itself is demanding their best;
(c) Must receive adequate recognition for their achievements;
(d) Must feel secure within the terms of reference;

131

(e) Must have control over those aspects of their job which have been delegated to them;

(f) Must feel that they as individuals are developing, that they are advancing in experience and ability.

Building the team

Although we are employed on the basis of individual contracts, it is in groups or teams that the majority of our work is conducted. A group exists as an entity and, as with individuals, no two groups are alike. A group has power to set its own standards of behaviour and performance and to impose them even when contrary to the interest of the individual and the organisation.

The successful supervisor understands that a group has its own personality, its own power, its own attitudes, its own standards and its own needs. You achieve your success by taking these things into account. You have constantly to respond to the needs of the group. At times this means withdrawing from your position 'way out front' and concentrating on 'serving those who service him'. On these occasions you must be prepared to represent the group and speak with its voice. At the same time avoid 'over-identifying'.

The key functions of the leader in meeting group needs are:

(a) To set and maintain group objectives and group standards;
(b) To involve the group as a whole in the achievement of objectives;
(c) To maintain the unity of the group and to see that dissident activity is minimised.[10]

Each of the three lists of team contributions is backed up by check lists (Appendix 9). The feedback from courses run using this model suggests that new senior probation officers have found it helpful and it may well be a useful starting-point for experienced middle managers wanting to review their supervisory process. However, care must always be taken when giving a model to inexperienced staff. At this point in their professional development the offer of a 'painting by numbers' package of leadership can be very tempting for some. This is not what Adair was suggesting of course, but his model could be abused in this way. For example the three areas of need illustrated in the diagram do not highlight the need for middle managers to play a part in the development of service task and practice. It could be simplistically interpreted in such a way as to suggest that middle managers receive their aims, objectives and targets from above and set about the task of getting the team to achieve these goals. Such an approach might offer short-term satisfaction but could cause problems in the long-term if the middle manager is not feeding back views, suggestions and trends to senior management.

Model eight — supervisory modes

The South West Regional Staff Development Unit has produced a further model which breaks down the process of supervision into six modes.[11] This is a helpful model as it gives indicators of when each mode is likely to be needed, suggests a style for operating in each mode, gives clues as to the likely consequences of operating in each, and finally suggests the key skills which supervisors need to operate in each mode. The six modes suggested are:

1 Educating
2 Coaching
3 Counselling
4 Sponsoring
5 Negotiating
6 Confronting.

Thus the answer to the question 'what is supervision?' is revealed as follows:

Educate

Timing   When objectives, roles or conditions change. To orient a new-comer. When you are new to group. When new skills are needed.
Tone   Positive, supportive. Emphasis on learning and applying specific new knowledge.
Consequences   New skills acquired. Confidence increases. Perspective on the organisation is broadened.
Key skills   Ability to articulate performance expectations clearly. An eye for recognising real life learning moments. Ability and willingness to reinforce learning.

Coach

Timing   For special encouragement before or after a 'first'. To make simple brief corrections.
Tone   Encouraging, enthusiastic, preparatory, explanatory.
Consequences   Enhanced confidence, skills, better performance.
Key skills   Ability to express genuine appreciation. Ability to listen.

Counsel

Timing   When problems damage performance. To respond to setbacks and disappointments and speed recovery.
Tone   Emphasis on problem solving. Positive, supportive, encouraging, structured. Two-way discussion.
Consequences   Turn around. Enhanced sense of ownership and accountability. Renewed commitment.
Key skills   Willingness to listen. Ability to give clear useful feedback.

Sponsor

Timing   When an individual can make a special contribution. To let an outstanding skill speak for itself.
Tone   Positive, enthusiastic. Emphasis on long-term development. Future focus. Polishing, fine-tuning.
Consequences   Showcase for outstanding skill, contribution, greater experience. Promotion.
Key skills   Dismantle barriers to performance. Willingness to let go of control. Willingness to provide access to information and people.

Negotiate

Timing   When private opportune moment appears. When change is required and no agreed solution is evident.
Tone   Conciliatory/threatening. Friendly/aggressive. Reflective/open.
Consequences   Change of working practice. Enhanced recognition. New rules and/or relationships.
Key skills   Listening, patience, empathy. Knowing when to retreat.

Confront

Timing   Persistent performance problems are not resolved. Individual seems unable to meet expectations despite educating and counselling.
Tone   Positive, supportive, firm. Clear focus on need for decision. Calm.
Consequences   Improved performance, reassignment. Another role, current job restructured. Dismissal.
Key skills   Listening, ability to give direct, useful feedback. Knowledge of agreed procedures. Ability to discuss sensitive issues without overemotionalising them.

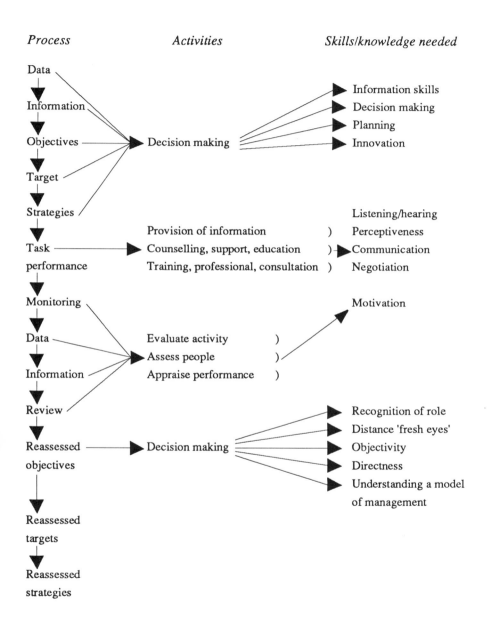

| Process | Activities | Skills/knowledge needed |

Process

Data

Information

Objectives

Target

Strategies

Task

performance

Monitoring

Data

Information

Review

Reassessed
objectives

Reassessed
targets

Reassessed
strategies

Activities

Decision making

Provision of information)
Counselling, support, education)
Training, professional, consultation)

Evaluate activity)
Assess people)
Appraise performance)

Decision making

Skills/knowledge needed

Information skills
Decision making
Planning
Innovation

Listening/hearing
Perceptiveness
Communication
Negotiation

Motivation

Recognition of role
Distance 'fresh eyes'
Objectivity
Directness
Understanding a model
of management

Figure 5.7

135

Model nine — information systems as an aid to supervision

A working party set up in 1985 to look at the training needs of managers regarding staff supervision produced a number of models including the one described in Figure 5.7 (p. 135), which is the work of Colin Roberts, Regional Staff Development Officer for the Midlands region, and Martin Seddon, Assistant Chief Probation Officer, Hereford and Worcester probation service.[12] This model emphasises the need for supervisors to have a high quality information system and to develop the skills required to use accurate data to assess task and practice. They stress the need to be clear about the supervisory process, which they see as a continual process of assessment and re-assessment. They also highlight the activities a middle manager should be involved in if the process is to be effective and lastly they suggest the skills and knowledge that a supervisor is likely to need to be suitably equipped to carry out the task. The process is diagrammatically described in Figure 5.7.

Model ten — pivotal supervision

Jenny Guise (SPO West Midlands) has produced a model for senior probation officers which encourages teams to be more responsible for their own effectiveness and development whilst the senior develops skills at representing the views of field staff to senior management and vice versa.[13] Effective two-way communication through the line management system is crucial to the probation service and this model suggests strongly that the senior probation officer is the pivot for such communication. Such an approach could not be installed overnight as teams need to develop support and development systems whilst assistant chiefs must also encourage teams of seniors to share

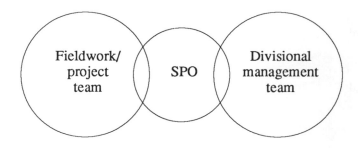

Figure 5.8

accountability for what is happening in the divisional team rather than the normal arrangement which tends to leave individual seniors feeling accountable for what happens in *their* team. Once again the model in its simplest form is best described diagrammatically (see Figure 5.8).

If lists of the tasks for the team supervisor in Figure 5.8 were drawn they would include those listed in Table 5.2.

Table 5.2

Team	SPO	Divisional management team
Manages throughput of work SPO: — through leadership facilitates team ownership of responsibility for effectiveness of work — elicits individual and shared skills — facilitates development of strategies to meet needs. — fosters team supervision of staff, also supervising at an individual level where appropriate — keeps in touch with team's needs and developments through limited practice.	Is accountable to divisional management team for team's function and performance Represents team to divisional management team and vice versa. Interprets agency policy to team. Seeks to inform divisional management team of areas of policy team would like to influence. Obtains resources for teams.	SPO shares divisional management team accountability for effective deployment and development of resources to meet division's responsibilities. A sharing not a competitive forum. Agrees divisional policy for interpreting agency policy. Seeks to inform and influence CMT. Is accountable for maintaining and monitoring standards.

Model eleven — live supervision

Live supervision has been attempted in a number of probation teams in recent years but has not so far been picked up with any enthusiasm by the service generally. This is surprising as the problem of supervisors relying on the reading of records followed by discussions based on information derived from case recording is often raised. There is clearly much that can be left out of a case recording or misinterpreted by the recorder. The worker's supervisor can then be selective or misinterpret the recording, thus leaving the eventual discussion far removed from what is actually happening to the client and worker in the case.

It is interesting to note that the shortcomings of this approach are acknowledged in training establishments, and social work students are often asked to be involved in much more rigorous supervisory processes. The practice teacher may ask for interviews to be audio-taped or placed on video for assessment. The practice teacher may well also ask to be allowed to 'sit in' on interviews. However, on appointment to the service officers are rarely asked to be involved in similar exercises although this research suggests that most staff would not be unhappy if suggestions along these lines were made. It seems that despite being aware of the shortcomings of relying on records on which to base supervision we are content to do this rather than look for ways of bringing supervision to life.

So what is live supervision? Jenny Guise is also an advocate of live supervision and she describes the process as follows: 'At its simplest it is the involvement at first hand of 2 workers in an interview, each with agreed defined roles and responsibilities.'[14] However, it is not a simple process. The two workers concerned need to discuss at length the objectives of such an approach and how they feel about embarking on it. Roles and boundaries need to be established and the workers must have confidence in each other — the confidence that provides a feeling of safety but also the confidence that both will be able to discuss openly and frankly with each other. Donna Smith and Philip Kingston[15] have produced the following useful check list for those considering using live supervision:

Basis for live consultation/supervision

1 *Before agreeing to work together*, check whether there is:
   (a) a reasonable congruence of models/style (check by discussing cases).
   (b) a commitment to work at difficulties as openly as possible.
   (c) a belief that the consultant position offers a wider, more detached perception than does the therapist position.
   (d) an ability to deal with role-differences:
        of profession;
        of hierarchical level;
        of sex, age, colour, etc;
        in a functional way.

2 *General areas to work on:*
   (a) the right 'not to know' — to be incompetent.
   (b) developing experience in both roles.
   (c) agreeing the administrative and accountability aspects of the joint work.
   (d) agreeing to work together for a specified length of time, number of families etc.
   (e) (where there is a supervisor–supervisee relationship) the implications of formal assessment for their work together.

3 *Ground-rules for the session:*
   (a) a pro-session discussion.
   (b) one 'time-out' of limited duration and focus.

(c) either party to seek other 'times-out' (if feeling stuck; or losing a meta-position; or experiencing lack of congruence with partner).
(d) consultant to intervene usually via the therapist.
(e) consultant interventions to be focused and brief.
(f) the status of the consultant's intervention — 'must' or 'may'.
(g) seating arrangements.
(h) introductions to the family: who does them and how?
(i) agreeing a post-session discussion in which the family *and* the way the therapist worked together are discussed.
(j) (where there is a supervisor–supervisee relationship) the conditions under which a supervisor may take over the interview from a supervisee.

Using this approach can be threatening for both parties as it involves exposing skills and limitations, hence the need to ensure a healthy relationship between those involved. But the advantages are obvious. The consultant can 'feel' the level at which the worker is operating and how effectively. It is a genuine sharing of the worker's pressures and provides the opportunity for a realistic exchange of views at a later stage as to how to continue the work. The worker has the benefit of a second opinion based on real information rather than recorded snippets and an occasional summary.

Live supervision does not require the senior to automatically act as the consultant in these situations. In fact there are good arguments for the senior not to be the consultant — much will depend on the purpose of the supervision. However, it is an approach that appears to have considerable potential and senior probation officers may well find it useful to facilitate it when appropriate.

Model twelve — peer supervision

There have been a number of attempts at peer supervision within the service in past years. When tracing the history of staff supervision earlier reference was made to the article written by Green and Glanfield regarding 'the seniorless team'. The difficulty with this approach seems to lie in the area of accountability. Whilst peer supervision can offer much in terms of support and constructive criticism, those involved seem much less confident that accountability systems devised will 'hold up' in times of crisis. Many field staff feel vulnerable if their work has not been validated by management. It could be argued that if a supervisory process has been approved by a management then it has endorsed both the process and the quality of work produced by that process. However, in discussions with those involved in a degree of peer supervision, concern was expressed that

Table 5.3

Process	Content
The weekly team meeting	Looks at workload issues. Considers the systems working within the group. Reviews problematic cases.
Individual supervision 2 people each week via 2 sub-groups. The ratio of supervisee to 2 or 3 peer supervisors reduces the feeling of being 'in the hot seat'. Also speeds up the process. This way in a team of 8 each person will be supervised every 4 weeks.	Agenda items in these sessions can be very wide ranging under the general heading of supervisee's contribution to the team.
Group supervision Monthly meetings to consider how effectively the group is carrying out its tasks.	Focus could vary from an analysis of internal processes to a professional development session (e.g. dealing with violent casual callers).
Informal supervision To aid teamwork and quality of service to clients all 'C' sheets are held centrally; thus the duty officer has up-to-date information on all clients.	Informal supervision is thereby informed by easy access to all team members' records, encouraging the sharing of problems and styles of working.
Evaluation procedures The team writes an evaluation on individuals at the appropriate time. Comments are then added by the senior, and in due course, by the assistant chief.	Much of the evaluation document is derived from the supervision sessions held. At evaluation time an individual may well have a supervision session that focuses on the forthcoming evaluation.

this could be little more than a cosmetic exercise that fell apart if problems emerged, leaving individuals vulnerable.

To cope with the problem of accountability those that see peer supervision as the way forward often adjust the senior role towards an inspectorial function which may well be appropriate if sounder ways of checking quality of work than the traditional reading of records can be found.

There are other problems that emerge when this model is embarked upon. Comments made suggest that whilst criticism from a line manager may be hard to cope with on occasions, it is much easier than being the 'victim' of a group discussion in which several peer groups members centre on a particular weakness. Also, there is the question of time. If all staff want weekly supervision the team could spend half its working life in such meetings! Furthermore there is the question of change. Most teams have one or two personnel changes annually and these changes can be very hard to accommodate if a team approach to supervision is operating. Lastly there is the question of the use made of supervision. Will notes be kept? Who has access to them? Will they be used as the basis for future references by management? Should they be used?

Clearly there are many problems but those interested in developing this model of supervision are aware that the task is not easy. Finding a process for a team can take years and even then must be able to cope with adjustment as situations change. The benefits for those who find an acceptable model can be attractive. During this research those operating peer supervision in some degree report a feeling of being strongly supported, highly motivated and professionally stretched.

A model using information from two areas using peer supervision is illustrated in Table 5.3. It attempts to resolve some of the problems mentioned but as with any process snags can still be found and any service wishing to develop this approach would need to take local issues and structures into account.

Notes

1   Payne and Scott, *Developing Supervision of Teams in Field and Residential Social Work, Part I*, NISW paper no. 12, 1982.
2   East Midlands Probation Services, *Staff Supervision: Care and Control?*, NAPO, 1986.
3   Payne and Scott, *Developing Supervision of Teams in Field and Residential Social Work, Part I*, NISW paper no. 12, 1982.
4   Ibid.
5   Watson, Kenneth, 'Differential Supervision', *Journal of Social Work*, November 1973.
6   Cohen, Yona, 'Staff supervision in probation', *Federal Probation*, September 1976.
7   Ibid.
8   Tibbert, J., unpublished, 'Styles of Staff Supervision'.
9   Adair, John, *Effective Leadership (A modern guide to developing leadership skills)*, Pan Books (Business/Management), 1983.
10   South West Regional Staff Development Unit.
11   Ibid.
12   Roberts, C. and Seddon, M., 'Staff Supervision Working Party Discussion Starter', unpublished, 1986.
13   Guise, Jenny, 'Staff Supervision Working Party Discussion Starter', unpublished, 1986.
14   Guise, Jenny, 'West Midlands Probation Service', 1985.
15   Smith, Donna and Kingston, Philip, 'West Midlands Probation Service', unpublished.

6 Conclusions

Judging from the response rate to the questionnaires (90 per cent) and the enthusiasm, interest and depth of thinking demonstrated by those interviewed during this research it seems fair to conclude that the subject of staff supervision in the probation service is currently considered a very important one. Officers from all grades present are concluding that developments within the service generally have outpaced our supervisory processes and that the time has come to review the nature of the supervisory task and how it is carried out.

This research does not prompt the author to startling new conclusions but it may assist to clarify some issues, provide evidence to add weight to some of the notions put forward about staff supervision, and pull together some of the thinking that has been taking place across the ten probation services that make up the Midlands region. The author has certainly learnt a great deal about the subject whilst researching it and gives below a list of conclusions reached. As with most research, many of the conclusions are likely to raise more questions than answers. For some services the conclusions may not apply. It is hoped that if the reader sees conclusions that ring bells regarding his/her service, he/she will pursue the questions that are raised. If this happens it will hopefully improve the chances of individual services finding a supervisory process that meets its particular, unique requirements.

1   Almost everybody involved in this research feels that both the

quality and quantity of supervision should and could be improved. Many people feel guilty about their part of the process, believing they are not doing justice to an important aspect of our service. The reasons why we are not achieving the standards we aspire to are many and varied — lack of resources, training, organisational growth and diversification, etc. Staff at all levels should be encouraged to acknowledge any weaknesses in their supervisory processes. Far too many people at all levels give the impression that to acknowledge all is not well is to acknowledge a personal failure. Thus debate regarding the problems of staff supervision is suppressed and the information managements need to improve the situation is not available.

2   Staff supervision, which began as a relatively simple exercise sixty years ago has now become an extremely complex task. While much has been added to the task, little appears to have been removed. Supervisors now supervise resources, information systems, projects, professional practice and workload management, as well as being responsible for service development and the encouragement of new initiatives. There may well be scope for moving away from the standard probation team with a supervisor acting as jack of all trades with his/her team of six or seven workers.

3   When supervision is effective one of the vital ingredients is that both supervisor and supervisee see the interaction as relevant to the current objectives and needs of those involved. This means that to keep the process 'alive' there must be regular planned reviews. The review must include a management perspective, team perspective and an individual perspective. This applies to all staff regardless of grade. The senior that reviews his objectives and needs solely with his assistant chief probation officer without reference to the team does so at his peril.

4   Supervisor and supervisees should agree a framework for the supervisory process. Most people in the service are part of a small group or team and normally the framework would be part of an overall team model for staff supervision. Supervisees should not be subjected to haphazard unrecorded supervisory sessions without agendas, or themes emerging. A good framework provides an opportunity to share important aspects of the supervisees' work. Without a framework supervisees are subjected to stresses which are not properly shared and dealt with. Those stresses accumulate and will eventually be expressed by dysfunction which will in turn depress the worker. This is disastrous in a service such as ours which is so often faced with a depressed clientele. To quote Cohen: 'The probation officers optimism is in itself a factor conducive to success'.[1]

5   Line management at all levels should be involved in reviews of staff supervision. Team reviews which produce a new process eventually validated by management are not good enough. Reviews of supervisory processes are difficult and likely to require lengthy discussions. Often these discussions involve subtle negotiations which senior managers must 'own' if the process is to survive difficult situations. The roles and responsibilities of staff at all grades should be clear, together with the role of team meetings. It is particularly important that boundary lines and accountability issues are clarified and agreed at all levels.

6   Whilst statements of national and local objectives and priorities have made a considerable impact on staff, particularly in terms of the focus of supervision, there are dangers. These statements appear to have been particularly helpful in moving the focus of supervision and evaluation away from the personal pathology model towards task appraisal. However, the pressure on supervisors to concentrate on achieving targets and priorities could encourage a one-way, 'top down', approach to supervision. Whilst in the short term middle managers adopting a policy-monitoring role could be seen as striving to 'deliver the goods', in the long term the failure to communicate accurately fieldwork views and issues could lead to 'out of touch' senior management. If middle managers fail to develop a good two-way communication system, opting for the policy-monitoring role, an essential line management link will be weakened which could lead to a clear 'them and us' division in the long term.

7   Even now there still seems to be considerable fudging of the fundamental differences between consultations and supervision. Many supervisors still see themselves operating as consultants to their staff. This creates difficulties when a failure to agree emerges. The subordinate feels he has professional freedom to disagree, the superior disagrees and invokes line superiority. The subordinate feels betrayed. The same problem often emerges when supervisors and supervisees confuse consultations with participative decision making.

All those involved in this research acknowledged the need for accountability systems and that authority be invested in a line management system. It seems to be the timid manner in which many supervisors accept that authority that usually creates the problems. No doubt the non-directive philosophy of the service contributes to the desire of supervisors to do the 'nice' consultations and to avoid the 'nasty' inspectorial aspects. However, supervisors need not be so timid. This research suggests that supervisees would welcome more clarity. They want to know if they are participating in decision making, being consulted, inspected or simply being told what to do.

8   Many field probation officers are concerned regarding the developments of the senior probation officer role. Indeed it is fair to say that many senior officers are concerned about their role. Probation officers expressed anxiety regarding the reduced importance apparently being attached to the supervision of their casework. They feel that at a time when the service is being asked to work with high-risk cases there should be more time spent with officers, supporting and validating their casework, not less. There is sympathy for the senior officer under pressure to develop community links, co-ordinate resources more efficiently and match them to service objectives, develop projects, etc., but this sympathy is tempered with a feeling of being used to make supervisors look good at the expense of supporting and developing good professional practice. The question often asked at field level is:

> If senior probation officers are to become full-time resource managers and policy monitors who is going to help me develop my practice skills and validate my work with an increasingly difficult caseload?

9   The majority of staff whilst feeling there is room for improvement do find the supervision they receive helpful. However, for a few supervision has become a battleground. Working in the probation service is a stressful business and all staff have a right to a helpful supervisory process. Unfortunately when conflict emerges between supervisor and supervisee the service seems somewhat unimaginative in its response. Some interviewees talked about the need for people to 'work through' their conflict, sometimes quite unrealistically. In other situations the line system seemed to unquestioningly support the supervisor, thus labelling the supervisee troublesome. This is a very powerful weapon as it can destroy careers, therefore officers are under pressure to toe the line or keep quiet regarding bad practice on the part of some supervisors. It must be remembered that this is a concern of a minority group, but for these people their professional life becomes almost intolerable. They are being asked to cope with a stressful task without feeling they have managerial support or that they are valued. Perhaps services could give some thought to this subject and find a few more options when faced with conflict of this kind.

10   Supervisory grades within the service feel that staff supervision has more impact on staff than field probation officers, who

consider that the process has some effect but not a great deal. This is perhaps not surprising and when looked at in greater detail the point is arguable. Nevertheless there are different perceptions on the impact between supervisors and supervisees. Individual services may find it useful to explore the reasons for this. For example it may be that service management objectives do not match field staff objectives. Thus supervisors and supervisees find it hard to agree a mutually relevant agenda. Alternatively it could be that the supervision provided lacks credibility or that staff are simply not receptive to supervision for various reasons.

11   The development of specialists and specialisms requires the service to think carefully about the needs of these workers and how their work is to be integrated into the mainstream operation. Who is to offer support and professional development opportunities to specialist staff? The line manager may well not have the experience or knowledge to provide this. At the same time the provision of these supervisory facilities needs to be carefully arranged and agreed. If they are not the line manager may well feel threatened or undermined. Furthermore supervisors need to develop their skills and confidence in using specialists in a consultant capacity with their staff if specialists are to maximise their value to the organisation.

12   In most cases the recording of supervision is of poor quality or non-existent at present, despite a generally held view that good quality recording would be a valuable aid to the process. This situation is likely to remain unless individual services give the matter a high priority and find the time and resources to formulate service guidelines. At present those who might be keen to develop recording are faced with a daunting number of dilemmas, regarding the content, style and status of any recording they may undertake.

13   There seems to be a great deal of supervision undertaken under the heading of 'informal supervision'. For many supervisors it seems acceptable to slip into the informal supervision mode from a social chat in a car or over lunch. However, many field staff are alarmed at this and become defensive after experiencing such an event. Many officers become cautious when they realise that coffee-room conversations can become formal supervision agenda items. Some are not made aware that such conversations are sometimes used elsewhere. Clearly this is a minefield and a rigid approach may well prove harmful. However, services may find it helpful to discuss the notion of informal supervision. What is it? How should it be used? In particular it might be worth

exploring its use as a 'catch all' insurance policy by poor supervisors. Similarly it may be helpful to explore the real value of the alleged 'open door policy' claimed by many supervisors. 'Is this a genuine facility for staff or an insurance policy for supervisors?'

14 Staff supervision at present lacks consistency. The style of supervisors and the objectives of the task, as they see it, usually reflect the experiences so far of the supervisor. Not only is this not good enough from the service's point of view, it is grossly unfair on supervisees. An important conclusion emerged from the research that had not been part of the original research thinking or objectives. Returned questionnaires and interviews regularly referred to supervision as a lottery — that a great deal depended on the supervisor and supervisee 'getting on'. Many people had experienced personal evaluations which were glowing if they had a good relationship with their supervisor and highly critical if there was conflict within the relationship. Whilst it would be unrealistic to attempt to eliminate subjective feelings from the supervisory process many people interviewed felt that a review of what actually takes place under the heading of supervision could lead to a reduction of the lottery element.

15 It is probably both undesirable and unrealistic to separate the supervisory process from the staff evaluation process. However, the evaluation process can be an extremely powerful controller of staff. Services may well be able to find ways of dealing with this situation that will enhance open and frank exchanges of views within the supervisory process. Clarity of procedures and criteria coupled with consistency could go a long way to easing this problem.

Overall there appear to be many problems within the service's supervisory processes at present but as described in Chapter 2 this has always been the case and will continue to be so. As the service task practice and personnel change, the problems will change and processes to deal with them must change. There is much to be optimistic about. Most people already find the process helpful, staff at all levels are motivated towards improving the situation and there is currently considerable interest in developing the quality of staff supervision provided.

The service has always prided itself on its ability to accommodate a broadly-based staff group with a wide range of previous experiences, philosophies and approaches to the task. It has managed to develop quickly throughout this century by allowing open debate, a free exchange of views and working towards consensus decision making.

It has moved from the days of independent freelancing into professional organisations without becoming unduly authoritarian or bureaucratic. These are achievements that should not be undervalued. They can be built on. However, as the service grows the possibility of an authoritarian 'top down' approach, and/or a bureaucratic approach will regularly become attractive when the service is under stress. It offers tidiness. It offers order. But the probation service operates in the messiest part of a messy society and the rules keep changing. Therefore it needs to encourage flair, perseverance, commitment and motivation. It also needs to encourage a good communication system that enables staff at all levels to hear each other.

This is why the service needs good quality staff supervision. There is agreement across all grades regarding its basic components. However, perhaps the most important component of staff supervision is simply that it is a line of communication within the service. The style of that communication is vital regarding service development. If it becomes a top down style in which ideas and policy emanate from above (i.e. the Home Office), supervisors become policy monitors and field staff become policy implementors, we run the risk of becoming in the short term a confused argumentative service. In the medium term we could become a dull, unimaginative mildly controlling agency, and in the long term we may disappear altogether.

If, however, the service uses staff supervision imaginatively; if it is used to encourage new ideas; if it is used to encourage an exchange of views and involve staff at all levels in the future directions of the service; if staff feel the supervision they receive is relevant to their task and to their aspirations for the service; if they feel they will be supported by their managers in their efforts, then the basic unity of purpose that has kept the service healthy throughout this century will remain intact. The service will remain lively, pioneering a range of responses to offending that command respect from all sections of the community.

Staff supervision has been adequate for most people in the service since supervisory grades were first introduced. For some it has been inspirational, for a few others sadly it has been poor or non-existent. However, the time has come for review. Objectives and priorities have been reassessed. Targets are being set. The service is now looking at how to achieve these objectives and where we go from here. An important part of that equation is how we supervise a talented committed staff striving to improve the quality of service to those we serve.

Note

1   Cohen, Y., 'Staff supervision in probation', *Federal Probation*, 1976.

148

APPENDICES

Appendix 1 The pilot questionnaires

My thanks for agreeing to complete the attached pilot questionnaire.

I am currently undertaking some research into staff supervision and intend sending out these questionnaires to 300 probation staff later in the year. However, I am aware that some refinements are probably required. Therefore I would be most grateful if you could attach any remarks regarding the questionnaire design to the completed questionnaire before returning it. Feedback regarding the pilot questionnaire is vital.

The questionnaire itself should not take many minutes to complete. Where applicable, I would be grateful if you could record what is your normal practice, not what you would do in an ideal world. Obviously it is impossible to be precise, each supervisory arrangement tends to be unique. Nevertheless I am hoping that if responses reflect normal practice it will give me an outline of the state, or should I say the art, of staff supervision in the service.

CHIEF OFFICER GRADES QUESTIONNAIRE

1. How long have you been in your present post? _____ years

2. Do you provide regular formal supervision to your staff? Yes/No
    (If not ignore question 3)

3. How often do you regularly formally supervise the following?

	Weekly	Fortnightly	Monthly	Bi-monthly	Quarterly	Annually	Never
1st years SPO's	☐	☐	☐	☐	☐	☐	☐
More experienced SPO's	☐	☐	☐	☐	☐	☐	☐
1st year officers	☐	☐	☐	☐	☐	☐	☐
More experienced officers	☐	☐	☐	☐	☐	☐	☐
1st year assistants	☐	☐	☐	☐	☐	☐	☐
More experienced assistants	☐	☐	☐	☐	☐	☐	☐
1st year administrative staff	☐	☐	☐	☐	☐	☐	☐
More experienced administrative staff	☐	☐	☐	☐	☐	☐	☐

4. Do you receive formal supervision? Yes/No (If not ignore questions 5 and 6)

5. From whom do you receive formal supervision?

CPO	ACPO colleagues	Home Office	My SPO's	Outside consultants
☐	☐	☐	☐	☐

6. How often are you formally supervised?

Weekly	Fortnightly	Monthly	Bi-monthly	Quarterly	Annually	Never
☐	☐	☐	☐	☐	☐	☐

152

7. There are many possible objectives linked to 'formal supervision'. Twelve are listed below. Please rank them in the order of importance you think they should be given.

a) Stimulating thought about the task and widening horizons regarding the options that are available. [ ]

b) The monitoring of work for research purposes. [ ]

c) To act as insurance for staff. Protection against criticism. 'My superior knew and agreed with me'. [ ]

d) To act as insurance for management. Protection against criticism. 'I advised him/her not to do it'. [ ]

e) Identifying training needs. [ ]

f) Ensuring service minimum standards of practice are adhered to. [ ]

g) Providing professional support for staff. [ ]

h) An opportunity for staff to share their problems. [ ]

j) Ensuring staff accountability to the service. [ ]

k) To provide a second opinion in difficult situations. [ ]

l) Provision of information needed by management for future planning and development. [ ]

m) To promote consistency and fairness for users to the service. [ ]

If you can identify other important objectives please list them below.

8. Do you feel that supervision has any impact ? Yes/No
   (If answer is no please move on to question 10)

9. What effect do you consider staff supervision has ? (Please tick as many boxes below as you wish).

	A LITTLE	A GREAT DEAL
Improves the quality of work staff undertake	☐	☐
Places staff under more pressure	☐	☐
Clarifies thought	☐	☐
Makes people more enthusiastic about task	☐	☐
Changes professional practice	☐	☐
Depresses people	☐	☐
Stimulates people	☐	☐
Encourages staff to share their problems	☐	☐
Encourages staff to hide their problems	☐	☐

If there are any other effects you would like to mention please list them below.

10. Do you feel that any of the following 6 points have changed the nature of staff supervision? (Please tick as many boxes as you wish).

	NO	A LITTLE	A GREAT DEAL
a) The growing emphasis on working with 'high risk' offenders in the community.	☐	☐	☐
b) The growth of projects within the service and the degree to which staff are expected to develop projects.	☐	☐	☐
c) The changing and developing roles of staff in the service.	☐	☐	☐
d) The growing emphasis on packages within probation orders that commit clients and staff to tighter contracts with courts.	☐	☐	☐

154

	NO	A LITTLE	A GREAT DEAL
e) The movement towards a teamwork approach to fieldwork.	☐	☐	☐
f) The trend towards local statements of objectives and priorities.	☐	☐	☐

If you feel anything else has changed the nature of supervision please describe briefly below.

11. Have you reviewed your supervisory process during the last:

Year	2 years	5 years	10 years	Ever	Never
☐	☐	☐	☐	☐	☐

12. If you have reviewed your supervisory process who was involved in the review?

CPO	ACPO colleagues	My SPO's	Field teams	Home Office	Outside consultants
☐	☐	☐	☐	☐	☐

13. Are there any interesting developments regarding staff supervision concerning you or your area? If yes please describe briefly below.

SENIOR PROBATION OFFICERS QUESTIONNAIRE

1. How long have you been in the service? _____ years

2. How long have you been a Senior Probation Officer? _____ years

3. Do you operate a formal pre-arranged supervision system with your staff? Yes/No

(If the answer to this question is no please give more detailed information in the space below and ignore question 4).

4. How often do you provide formal supervision? Please tick boxes where appropriate in the table below.

	Never	Weekly	Fortnightly	Monthly	Bi-monthly	Quarterly	½ Yearly	Annually
1st year officers	☐	☐	☐	☐	☐	☐	☐	☐
1st to 3rd officers	☐	☐	☐	☐	☐	☐	☐	☐
3+ years officers	☐	☐	☐	☐	☐	☐	☐	☐
1st year probation assistants	☐	☐	☐	☐	☐	☐	☐	☐
1st to 3rd year probation assistants	☐	☐	☐	☐	☐	☐	☐	☐
3+ years probation assistants	☐	☐	☐	☐	☐	☐	☐	☐

5. Do you receive formal pre-arranged supervision? Yes/No

156

6. If yes, who supervises your work? Please tick as many boxes as appropriate

My ACPO   My CPO   My Team   My Colleagues   Others

☐   ☐   ☐   ☐   ☐

7. How often do you receive formal supervision?

Weekly   Fortnightly   Monthly   Bi-monthly   Quarterly   1/2 Yearly   Annually

☐   ☐   ☐   ☐   ☐   ☐   ☐

8. There are many possible objectives linked to 'formal supervision'. Twelve are listed below. Please rank them in the order of importance you think they should be given.

a) Stimulating thought about the task and widening horizons regarding the options that are available. ☐

b) The monitoring of work for research purposes. ☐

c) To act as insurance for staff. Protection against criticism. 'My superior knew and agreed with me'. ☐

d) To act as insurance for management. Protection against criticism. 'I advised him/her not to do it'. ☐

e) Identifying training needs. ☐

f) Ensuring service minimum standards of practice are adhered to. ☐

g) Providing professional support for staff. ☐

h) An opportunity for staff to share problems. ☐

j) Ensuring staff accountability to the service. ☐

k) To provide a second opinion in difficult situations. ☐

l) Provision of information needed by management for future planning and development. ☐

m) To promote consistency and fairness for users of the service. ☐

If you can identify other important objectives please list them below.

9. Do you feel that formal supervision has any impact? Yes/No
   (If answer is no please move to question 11.)

10. What effect do you consider formal staff supervision has?
    (Please tick as many boxes below as you wish.)

	NO	A LITTLE	A GREAT DEAL
Improves the quality of work staff undertake	☐	☐	☐
Places staff under more pressure	☐	☐	☐
Clarifies thought	☐	☐	☐
Makes people more enthusiastic about task	☐	☐	☐
Changes professional practice	☐	☐	☐
Depresses people	☐	☐	☐
Stimulates people	☐	☐	☐
Encourages staff to share problems	☐	☐	☐
Encourages staff to hide problems	☐	☐	☐

If there are any other effects you would like to mention please list them below.

11. Do you feel that any of the following 6 points have changed the nature
    of staff supervision? (Please tick as many boxes as you wish).

	NO	A LITTLE	A GREAT DEAL
a) The growing emphasis on working with 'high risk' offenders in the community.	☐	☐	☐
b) The growth of projects within the service and the degree to which staff are expected to develop projects.	☐	☐	☐
c) The changing and developing roles of staff in the Service.	☐	☐	☐

d)   The growing emphasis on packages
     within probation orders that commit
     clients and staff to tighter contracts
     with courts.

e)   The movement towards a teamwork
     approach to fieldwork.

f)   The trend towards local statements
     of objectives and priorities.

If you feel anything else has changed the nature of the formal supervisory process you are
involved in please specify below.

12. Have you reviewed the formal supervisory process you operate within your team
     during the last:

     Year   2 years   5 years   10 years   Ever   Never

13. If you have reviewed the team's formal supervision processes who was
     involved in the review? (Please tick whichever boxes are appropriate).

     My CPO   My ACPO   My team   My SPO   Home   Outside
                                        colleagues   Office   consultants

14. Have you reviewed the formal supervision you receive during the last:

     Year   2 years   5 years   10 years   Ever   Never

15. If the answer to question 14 is yes who was involved in the review?
     (Please tick as many boxes as appropriate)

     My CPO   My ACPO   My SPO   My team   Home   Outside
                             colleagues   Office   consultants

16. Are there any interesting developments regarding staff supervision concerning you and/ or your team at present?

If there are please describe briefly below.

FIELD STAFF QUESTIONNAIRE

1. How long have you been in the service?_____ years

2. Do you receive formal prearranged supervision of your work? Yes/No
    (If the answer is no please briefly describe the circumstances leading to this position
    below, then ignore questions 3, 4, 6 and 7).

3. Approximately how often do you receive formal supervisory sessions?

    Weekly   Fortnightly   Monthly   Bi-monthly   Quarterly   Half yearly   Annually
    ☐   ☐   ☐   ☐   ☐   ☐   ☐

4. Who supervises your work? (Please tick as many boxes as you wish)

    My SPO   My team   My ACPO   A colleague   Outside consultants
    ☐   ☐   ☐   ☐   ☐

5. There are many possible objectives linked to 'formal supervision'. Twelve are listed
    below. Please rank them in the order of importance you think they should be given.

a) Stimulating thought about the task and widening horizons
    regarding the options that are available.   ☐

b) The monitoring of work for research purposes.   ☐

c) To act as insurance for staff. Protection against criticism.
    'My superior knew and agreed with me'.   ☐

d) To act as insurance for management. Protection against
    criticism. 'I advised him/her not to do it'.   ☐

e) Identifying training needs. ☐

f) Ensuring service minimum standards of practice are adhered to. ☐

g) Providing professional support for staff. ☐

h) An opportunity for staff to share their problems ☐

j) Ensuring staff accountability to the service. ☐

k) To provide a second opinion in difficult situations. ☐

l) Provision of information needed by management for future planning and development. ☐

m) To promote consistency and fairness for users to the service. ☐

If you can identify other important objectives please list them below.

6. Does supervision have any effect on you? Yes / No

7. If the answer to question 6 is yes what effect does supervision have on you? (Please tick as many boxes as appropriate below).

	A LITTLE	A GREAT DEAL
a) Improves my work	☐	☐
b) Places me under more pressure	☐	☐
c) Clarifies my thoughts	☐	☐
d) Makes me more enthusiastic	☐	☐
e) Changes my professional practice	☐	☐
f) Depresses me	☐	☐
g) Makes me laugh	☐	☐
h) Encourages me to share problems	☐	☐
j) Encourages me to hide my problems	☐	☐

162

If formal supervision has other effects on you please describe below.

8. Do you feel that the 6 points listed below have changed the nature of the supervision you have been receiving? (Please tick as many boxes as you wish).

	NO	A LITTLE	A GREAT DEAL
a) The growing emphasis on working with 'high risk' offenders in the community.	☐	☐	☐
b) The growth of projects within the service and the degree to which staff are expected to develop projects.	☐	☐	☐
c) The changing and developing roles of staff in the service.	☐	☐	☐
d) The growing emphasis on packages within probation orders that commit clients and staff to tighter contracts with courts.	☐	☐	☐
e) The movement towards teamwork approaches to fieldwork.	☐	☐	☐
f) The trend towards local statements of objectives and priorities.	☐	☐	☐

If anything has changed the nature of your supervision please mention below.

9. Has your supervisory process been reviewed during the past.

Year	2 years	5 years	10 years	Ever	Never
☐	☐	☐	☐	☐	☐

10. If your supervisory process has been reviewed who was involved?
    (Please tick as many boxes as you wish).

My SPO	My team	My union	My ACPO	Outside consultants	Myself
☐	☐	☐	☐	☐	☐

11. To the best of your knowledge has your team reviewed staff supervision during the last

Year	2 years	5 years	10 years	Ever	Never
☐	☐	☐	☐	☐	☐

12. Are there any interesting developments regarding staff supervision concerning you or
    your team. If yes please describe briefly below.

164

Appendix 2 The finalised questionnaires

CHIEF OFFICER GRADES QUESTIONNAIRE

1. How long have you been in the Probation Service?

    Less than 15 years   Between 15 - 25 years   More than 25 years

    ☐   ☐   ☐

2. How long have you been in your present post?

Less than 1 year   Between 1 - 3 years   Between 3 - 5 years   Between 5 - 10 years   More than 10 years

    ☐   ☐   ☐   ☐   ☐

3. Do you provide regular formal supervision to your staff?   Yes ☐ No ☐
(If not ignore question 4)

4. How often do you regularly formally supervise the following?

	Weekly	Fortnightly	Monthly	Bi-monthly	Quarterly	Annually	Never	Not applicable
1st year SPO's	☐	☐	☐	☐	☐	☐	☐	☐
Other SPO's	☐	☐	☐	☐	☐	☐	☐	☐
1st year officers	☐	☐	☐	☐	☐	☐	☐	☐
Officers in first 3 years	☐	☐	☐	☐	☐	☐	☐	☐
Officers with more than 3 years	☐	☐	☐	☐	☐	☐	☐	☐
1st year assistants	☐	☐	☐	☐	☐	☐	☐	☐
Assistants in first 2 years	☐	☐	☐	☐	☐	☐	☐	☐
Assistants with more than 2 years	☐	☐	☐	☐	☐	☐	☐	☐

Adminis-   □   □   □   □   □   □   □   □
trative
staff

5. Do you receive formal supervision?   Yes □   No □
   (If not ignore questions 6 and 7)

6. From whom do you receive formal supervision?
   CPO   ACPO Colleagues   Home Office   My SPO's   Outside Consultants   Other
   □   □   □   □   □   □

7. How often are you formally supervised?
   Weekly   Fortnightly   Monthly   Bi-monthly   Quarterly   Annually   Never
   □   □   □   □   □   □   □

8. There are many possible objectives linked to 'formal supervision'. Ten are listed below.
   Please rank them in order of importance you think they should be given.

a) Stimulating thought about service tasks and widening horizons   □
   regarding the options that are available.

b) To act as insurance for staff and/or management. Protection   □
   against criticism. Should things go wrong.

c) Identifying training needs.   □

d) Ensuring service minimum standards of practice are adhered to.   □

e) Facilitating professional development.   □

f) An opportunity for staff to share their problems.   □

g) Ensuring staff accountability to the service.   □

h) To provide a second opinion in difficult situations.   □

i) Provision of information needed by management for future   □
   planning and development.

j) Contributing to on-going assessment of staff performance,   □
   providing material for staff evaluation.

9. If you can identify other important objectives please list them below.

166

10. What effect do you consider staff supervision has?

	None	A Little	A Great Deal
Improves the quality of work staff undertake	☐	☐	☐
Places staff under more pressure	☐	☐	☐
Clarifies thought	☐	☐	☐
Makes people more enthusiastic about task	☐	☐	☐
Changes professional practice	☐	☐	☐
Depresses people	☐	☐	☐
Stimulates people	☐	☐	☐
Encourages staff to share their problems	☐	☐	☐
Encourages staff to hide their problems	☐	☐	☐

11. Any other effects you would like to mention please list them below.

For office use

12. Do you feel that any of the following have changed the nature of staff supervision?

	No	A Little	A Great Deal
a) The growing emphasis on working with 'high risk' offenders in the community.	☐	☐	☐
b) The growth of projects within the service and the degree to which staff are expected to develop projects.	☐	☐	☐
c) The changing roles of staff in the service.	☐	☐	☐
d) The growing emphasis on packages within probation orders that commit clients and staff to tighter contracts with courts.	☐	☐	☐
e) The movement towards a teamwork approach to fieldwork.	☐	☐	☐
f) The trend towards local statements of objectives and priorities.	☐	☐	☐

167

13. If you feel anything else has changed that nature of supervision please describe briefly below.

For office use

14. Have you reviewed your supervisory process during the last:

Year	2 Years	5 Years	10 Years	Ever	Never
☐	☐	☐	☐	☐	☐

15. If you have reviewed your supervisory process who was involved in the review?

CPO	ACPO	Colleagues	My SPO's	Field Teams	Home Office	Outside Consultants
☐	☐	☐	☐	☐	☐	☐

16. Please briefly describe below any interesting developments regarding staff supervision concerning you or your areas.

For office use

Thank you very much for your assistance, please return this questionnaire in the enclosed stamped addressed envelope to:

Mr M D Davies
Senior Probation Officer
Derbyshire Probation Service HQ
18 Brunswood Road
Matlock Bath
MATLOCK
DE4 3PA

SENIOR PROBATION OFFICERS QUESTIONNAIRE

1. How long have you been in the Probation Service?

Less than 10 years   Between 10-5 years   Between 15-25 years   More than 25 years

☐   ☐   ☐   ☐

2. How long have you been a Senior Probation Officer?

Less than 1 year   Between 1-3 years   Between 3-5 years   Between 5-10 years   More than 10 years

☐   ☐   ☐   ☐   ☐

3. Do you operate a fomal pre-arranged supervision system with your staff?

Yes ☐   No ☐

(If the answer to this question is no please give more detailed information in the space below and ignore question 4).

For office use

☐
☐
☐
☐
☐

4. How often do you provide formal supervision? Please tick boxes where appropriate in the table below.

	Never	Weekly	Fortnightly	Monthly	Bi-monthly	Quarterly	¹/₂ Yearly	Annually	Not applicable
1st year officers	☐	☐	☐	☐	☐	☐	☐	☐	☐
Officers in 1st 3 years	☐	☐	☐	☐	☐	☐	☐	☐	☐
Officers with more than 3 years	☐	☐	☐	☐	☐	☐	☐	☐	☐
1st year assistants	☐	☐	☐	☐	☐	☐	☐	☐	☐
Assistants in first 2 years	☐	☐	☐	☐	☐	☐	☐	☐	☐
Assistants with more than 3 years	☐	☐	☐	☐	☐	☐	☐	☐	☐

5. Do you receive formal pre-arranged supervision? Yes ☐ No ☐

☐☐☐☐☐

6. If yes, who supervises your work? Please tick as many boxes as appropriate.

My ACPO   My CPO   My team   My colleagues   Outside consultants
☐   ☐   ☐   ☐   ☐

7. How often do you receive formal supervision?

Weekly   Fortnightly   Monthly   Bi-monthly   Quarterly   1/2 Yearly   Annually   Never
☐   ☐   ☐   ☐   ☐   ☐   ☐   ☐

8. There are many possible objectives linked to 'formal supervision'. Ten are listed below. Please rank them in the order of importance you think they should be given.

a) Stimulating thought about service task and widening horizons regarding the options that are available. ☐

b) To act as insurance for staff/or management should things go wrong. ☐

c) Identifying training needs. ☐

d) Ensuring service minimum standards of practice are adhered to. ☐

e) Facilitating professional development. ☐

f) An opportunity for staff to share problems ☐

g) Ensuring staff accountability to the service ☐

h) To provide a second opinion in difficult situations ☐

i) Provision of information needed by management for future planning and development ☐

j) Contributing to on-going assessment of staff performance, providing material for staff evaluation. ☐

9. If you can identify other important objectiveness please list them below.

For office use ☐☐☐☐

10. What effect do you consider formal staff supervision has?

	No	A little	A great deal
Improves the staff quality of work staff undertake	☐	☐	☐
Places staff under more pressure	☐	☐	☐
Clarifies thought	☐	☐	☐
Makes people more enthusiastic about task	☐	☐	☐
Changes professional practice	☐	☐	☐
Depresses people	☐	☐	☐
Stimulates people	☐	☐	☐
Encourages staff to share problems	☐	☐	☐
Encourages staff to hide problems	☐	☐	☐

11. If there are any other effects you would like to mention please list them below.

For office use ☐☐☐☐

12. Do you feel that any of the following have changed the nature of staff supervision?

	No	A little	A great deal
a) The growing emphasis on working with 'high risk' offenders in the community	☐	☐	☐
b) The growth of projects within the service and the degree to which staff are expected to develop projects.	☐	☐	☐
c) The changing roles of staff in the Service	☐	☐	☐
d) The growing emphasis on packages within probation orders that commit clients and staff to tighter contracts with courts.	☐	☐	☐
e) The movement towards a teamwork approach to fieldwork.	☐	☐	☐
f) The trend towards local statements of objectives and priorities.	☐	☐	☐

13. If you feel anything else has changed the nature of the formal supervisory process you are involved in please specify below.

14. Have you reviewed the formal supervisory process you operate within your team during the last:

Year	2 years	5 years	10 years	Ever	Never
☐	☐	☐	☐	☐	☐

15. If you have reviewed the teams formal supervisory processes who was involved in the review? (Please tick whichever boxes are appropriate)

My CPO	My ACPO	My team	My SPO colleagues	Home Office	Outside consultants
☐	☐	☐	☐	☐	☐

16. Have you reviewed the formal supervision you receive during the last:

Year	2 years	5 years	10 years	Ever	Never
☐	☐	☐	☐	☐	☐

17. If the answer to question 16 is yes who was involved in the review?
(Please tick as many boxes as appropriate)

My CPO	My ACPO	My SPO colleagues	My team	The Home Office	Outside consultants
☐	☐	☐	☐	☐	☐

18. Please briefly describe below any interesting developments regarding staff supervision concerning you or your areas. (Continue overleaf if appropriate)

Thank you very much for your assistance, please return the questionnaire in the enclosed, stamped addressed envelope to Mr M D Davies, Senior Probation Officer Derbyshire Probation Service, 18 Brunswood Road, Matlock Bath, MATLOCK, DE4 3PA.

CONFIDENTIAL

FIELD STAFF QUESTIONNAIRE

1. How long have you been in the Probation Service?

Less than 1 year   Between 1-3 years   Between 3-5 years   Between 5-10 years   More than 10 years

☐   ☐   ☐   ☐   ☐

2. Do you receive formal pre-arranged supervision of your work? Yes   No ☐   ☐
(If the answer is no please briefly describe the circumstances leading to this position below, then ignore questions, 3, 4, 6 and 7)

3. Approximately how often do you receive formal supervisory sessions?

Weekly   Fortnightly   Monthly   Bi-monthly   Quarterly   Half yearly   Annually

☐   ☐   ☐   ☐   ☐   ☐   ☐

4. Who supervises your work? (Please tick as many boxes as you wish)

My SPO   My team   My ACPO   A colleague   Outside consultants

☐   ☐   ☐   ☐   ☐

5. There are many possible objectives linked to 'formal supervision'. Ten are listed below. Please rank them in the order of importance you think they should be given.

a) Stimulating thought about service tasks and widening horizons regarding the options that are available.   ☐

b) To act as insurance for staff and/or management. Protection against criticism should things go wrong.   ☐

c) Identifying training needs.   ☐

d) Ensuring service minimum standards of practice are adhered to.   ☐

e) Facilitating professional development.   ☐

f) An opportunity for staff to share their problems.   ☐

g) Ensuring staff accountability to the service.   ☐

h) To provide a second opinion in difficult situations.   ☐

i) Provision of information needed by management for future planning and developing.   ☐

j) Contributing to on-going assessment of staff performance, providing material for staff evaluation   ☐

6. If you can identity other important objectives please list them below.

7. What effect does supervision have on you?

	No	A little	A great deal
Improves my work	☐	☐	☐
Places me under more pressure	☐	☐	☐
Clarifies my thoughts	☐	☐	☐
Makes me more enthusiastic	☐	☐	☐
Changes my professional practice	☐	☐	☐
Depresses me	☐	☐	☐
Stimulates me	☐	☐	☐
Encourages me to share problems	☐	☐	☐
Encourages me to hide my problems	☐	☐	☐

8. Any other effects you would like to mention please list them below.

9. Do you feel that any of the following have changed the nature of the supervision you have been receiving?

	No	A little	A great deal
a) The growing emphasis on working with 'high risk' offenders in the comunity	☐	☐	☐
b) The growth of projects within the service and the degree to which staff are expected to develop projects	☐	☐	☐
c) The changing roles of staff in the service	☐	☐	☐
d) The growing emphasis on packages within probation orders that commit clients and staff to tighter contracts with courts	☐	☐	☐
e) The movement towards teamwork approaches to fieldwork	☐	☐	☐
f) The trend towards local statements of objectives and priorities	☐	☐	☐

10. If anything else has changed the nature of your supervision please mention below.

For office use

11. Has your supervisory process been reviewed during the last:

Year	2 years	5 years	10 years	Ever	Never
☐	☐	☐	☐	☐	☐

12. If your supervisory process has been reviewed who was involved?
(Please tick as many boxes as you wish)

My SPO	My team	My union	My ACPO	Outside consultants	Myself
☐	☐	☐	☐	☐	☐

13. To the best of your knowledge has your team reviewed staff supervision during the last:

Year	2 years	5 years	10 years	Ever	Never
☐	☐	☐	☐	☐	☐

175

14. Please briefly describe below any interesting developments regarding staff supervision concerning you or your team.

Thank you very much for your assistance. Please return this questionnaire in the enclosed stamped adressed envelope to:

>Mr M D Davies
>Senior Probation Officer
>Derbyshire Probation Service
>18 Brunswood Road
>Matlock Bath
>MATLOCK
>DE4 3PA

Appendix 3 Letter to officers randomly selected to receive questionnaires

18 Brunswood Road, Matlock
Bath
Matlock, Derbyshire DE4 3PA
Telephone: Matlock 55422
Your reference:

My reference: MDD/LP

Date: 20 February 1986

Your Chief Probation Officer has kindly allowed me to contact you regarding a piece of research I am undertaking into staff supervision in the probation service. The objectives of the research are as follows:

1. To review the development of staff supervision in the probation service.

2. To obtain the views of staff as to the current purpose and nature of staff supervision in the service.

    The views obtained will be at three levels within the service, chief officer grades, senior probation officers and probation officers. Particular attention will be given to:

    a) The process of supervision
    b) What are the appropriate relationships? Who should supervise who?
    c) What are the different components of the supervisory exercise?
    d) What are the perceived objectives?
    e) What effect does it have?
    f) How do those involved feel about the process?

3. To explore the likely effects of recent developments in the service task and practice on staff supervision.

    Whilst other issues may emerge, particular attention will be given to considering :

    a) The growing emphasis on working with 'high risk' offenders in the community.
    b) The growth of project work within the service (eg day care, tracking schemes, reparation schemes).
    c) The changing and developing roles of staff at all levels.
    d) The trend towards developing 'packages' within probation orders that commit clients and staff to tighter contracts with courts than the basic probation order.
    e) The movement towards teamwork approach to tasks observable in many parts of the country.
    f) The influence of local Statements of Objectives and Priorities.

4. To consider the varying demands made of the supervisory process and explore models of supervision that may assist the service in its efforts to improve the quality of service delivery.

The research entails contracting 100 probation officers, 50 senior probation officers and 20 assistant chief probation officers, by way of random sample from the ten services that make up the Midlands region, and requesting the completion of a questionnaire. Your name has emerged as part of that sample, therefore I would be most grateful if you would complete and return the enclosed questionnaire. I am aware that your time is valuable and have attempted to make the questionnaire as simple as possible to complete. You will find that most questions only require a box to be ticked by way of reply. A pilot study has been carried out that suggests the questionnaire will take between ten and twenty minutes to complete.

The questionnaires have no identifying numbers therefore it will be impossible to identify individuals from completed questionnaires. The completed research will not only ensure that indviduals are not indentifiable, but also ensure that specific services are not identifiable. Where applicable, I would be grateful if you could record what is your normal practice, not what you would do in an ideal world. Obviously it is impossible to be precise, each supervisory arrangement tends to be unique. Nevertheless I am hoping that if responses reflect normal practice it will give me an outline of the state, or should I say the art, of staff supervision in the service.

If there are any matters you would like to discuss with me before returning the questionnaire please do not hesitate to give me a ring.

My thanks in advance for your valuable assistance in researching a subject that I believe will become increasingly important in the next few years.

Yours sincerely

M D Davies
Senior Probation Officer (Training)

Encl

Appendix 4 Reminder letter to participants

18 Brunswood Road, Matlock
Bath
Matlock, Derbyshire DE4 3PA
Telephone: Matlock 55422
Your reference:

My reference: MDD/LP

Date: 13 March 1986

Dear Mr

re: Staff Supervision In The Probation Service

Last week I sent you a questionnaire hoping you would find time to fill it in and return it. If you have been able to do this may I take this opportunity to thank you.

If you have not yet found space to complete the questionnaire could I take this chance to nudge your writing hand towards the questionnaire. It is vital to the credibility of my research that a good response is achieved across all grades.

If you have any queries, or if, by chance you have lost the questionnaire, please let me know and I will send a replacement copy.

Thank you for your help.

Yours sincerely

Mr M D Davies
Senior Probation Officer (Training)

Appendix 5 Aide memoire used by researcher when interviewing

STAFF SUPERVISION INTERVIEW AIDE MEMOIRE

1. Should senior probation officers move away from casework consultancy? Have they? Why? Who should fill the gap?

2. Is a record kept of your supervisory process?

3. What effect does change of superior have? How often does this happen? Is personality a key factor?

4. Evaluation issues. Should it be part of supervision? Who should evaluate who? Who should be involved? Who is involved?

5. What does team supervision mean?

6. What should the assistant chief probation officer role be in 'teamwork' and what are the implications for supervision?

7. Is it fair to say chief officers moving towards policy makers/ senior probation officers towards policy monitors/probation officers towards policy implementors? Comments re supervision.

8. What effect is specialisation having on the supervisory processes? Functional responsibility across boundaries.

9. Can supervision/consultation/management be separated?

10. How much teaching is required? Why?

Appendix 6 Likert questionnaire used to look at probation management systems as perceived by specialists

THE DEVELOPMENTS OF SPECIALISTS IN THE PROBATION SERVICE

I am currently undertaking some research into the development of specialists and specialisms in our service.

The attached questionnaire is commonly used to analyse the operating characteristics of organisations and is part of a process which places an organisation at one of 4 points known as the 'Likert' scale. Whilst the questionnaire looks lengthy it should only take a few minutes to complete as all that is required is a ring round the system of organisation that in your opinion applies in each of the areas listed in the column on the left. I would be most grateful if you could fill in the questionnaire and return it to me. All replies will be treated in confidence and I will be happy to provide you with a copy of the findings in due course if you so desire.

Please answer *all* questions giving *your* opinion.

ORGANIZATIONAL AND PERFORMANCE CHARACTERISTICS OF DIFFERENT MANAGEMENT SYSTEMS BASED ON A COMPARATIVE ANALYSIS

| Operating characteristics | SYSTEM OF ORGANIZATION | | | |
| | Authoritative | | Participative | |
	Exploitive authoritative	Benevolent authoritative	Consultative	Participative group
1 CHARACTER OF MOTIVATONAL FORCES				
1a) Underlying motives tapped	Physical security, economic security, and some use of the desire for status	Economic and occasionally ego motives, e.g. the desire for status	Economic, ego and other major motives e.g. desire for new experience	Full use of economic, ego, and other major motives, as, for example, motivational forces arising from group processes
1b) Manner in which motives are used	Fear, threats, punishment, and occasional rewards	Rewards and some actual or potential punishment	Rewards, occasional punishment, and some involvement	Economic rewards based on compensation system developed through participation. Group participation and involvement in setting goals, improving methods, appraising progress towards goals, etc.
1c) Satisfaction derived	Usually dissatisfaction with membership in the organization, with supervision, and with one's own achievements	Dissatisfaction to moderate satisfaction with regard to membership in the organization, supervision and one's own achievements	Some dissatisfaction to moderately high satisfaction with regard to membership in the organization, supervision, and one's own achievements	Relatively high satisfaction throughout the organization with regard to membership in the organization, supervision, and one's own achievements
2 CHARACTER OF COMMUNICATION PROCESS				
2a) Amount of interaction and communication aimed at achieving organization's objectives	Very little	Little	Quite a bit	Much with both individuals and groups
2b) Direction of information flow	Downward	Mostly downward	Down and up	Down, up, and with peers

182

2c) Down-ward com-munication				
1) Where initiated	At top of organization or to implement top directive	Primarily at top or patterned on communication from top	Patterned on communication from top but with some initiative at lower levels	Initiated at all levels
2) Extent to which com-munications are accepted by sub-ordinates	Viewed with great suspicion	May or may not be viewed with suspicion	Often accepted but at times viewed with suspicion. May or may not be openly questioned	Generally accepted, but if not, openly and candidly questioned
2d) Upward com-munication				
1) Adequacy of upward com-munication via line organization	Very little	Limited	Some	A great deal
2) Sub-ordinates' feeling of responsibility for initiating accurate upward com-munication	None at all	Relatively little, usually com-municates "filtered" information but only when re-quested. May "yes" the boss	Some to moderate degree of responsibility to initiate accurate upward com-munication	Considerable responsibility felt and much initiative. Group com-municates all relevant in-formation
3) Forces leading to accurate or distorted information	Powerful forces to distort in-formation and deceive superiors	Occasional forces to distort; also forces for honest com-munication	Some forces to distort along with many forces to communicate accurately	Virtually no forces to distort and powerful forces to communicate accurately
4) Accuracy of upward com-munication via line	Tends to be inaccurate	Information that boss wants to hear flows; other infor-mation is restricted and filtered	Information that boss wants to hear flows; other infor-mation may be limited or cautiously given	Accurate

3 CHARACTER OF INTERACTION — INFLUENCE PROCESS

3a) Amount and character of interaction	Little interaction and always with fear and distrust	Little interaction and usually with some con-descension by superiors; fear and caution by subordinates	Moderate interaction, often with fair amount of confidence and trust	Extensive, friendly inter-action with high degree of confidence and trust
3b) Amount of cooperative teamwork present	None	Virtually none	A moderate amount	Very substantial amount through-out the organization

Operating characteristics	SYSTEM OF ORGANIZATION			
	Authoritative		Participative	
	Exploitive authoritative	Benevolent authoritative	Consultative	Participative group
3c) Extent to which sub-ordinates can influence the goals, methods and activity of their units and depts				
1) As seen by superiors	None	Virtually none	Moderate amount	A great deal
2) As seen by sub-ordinates	None except through "informal organization" or via unionization	Little except through "informal organization" or via unionization	Moderate amount both directly and via unionization	Substantial amount both directly and via unionization
4 CHARACTER OF DECISION-MAKING PROCESS				
4a) At what level in organization are decisions formally made?	Bulk of decisions at top of organization	Policy at top, many decisions within prescribed framework made at lower levels	Broad policy and general decisions at top, more specific decisions at lower levels	Decision-making widely done throughout organization, although well integrated through linking process provided by over-lapping groups
4b) Extent to which technical and pro-fessional knowledge is used in decision making	Used only if possessed at higher levels	Much of what is available in higher and middle levels is used	Much of what is available in higher, middle, and lower levels is used	Most of what is available any-where within the organization is used
4c) Is decision making based on man-to-man or group pattern of operation? Does it en-courage or discourage teamwork?	Man-to-man only, discourages teamwork	Man-to-man almost entirely, discourages teamwork	Both man-to-man and group, partially en-courages teamwork	Largely based on group pattern, encourages teamwork
5 CHARACTER OF GOAL-SETTING OR ORDERING				
5a) Manner in which usually done	Orders issued	Orders issued, opportunity to comment may or may not exist	Goals are set or orders issued after discussion with sub-ordinate(s) of problems and planned action	Except in emergencies, goals are usually established by means of group participation

184

6 CHARACTER OF CONTROL PROCESSES

6a) Extent to which the review and control functions are concentrated	Highly concentrated in top management	Relatively highly concentrated, with some delegated control to middle and lower levels	Moderate downward delegation of review and control processes; lower as well as higher levels feel responsible	Quite widespread responsibility for review and control, with lower units at times imposing more rigorous reviews and tighter controls than top management

7 PERFORMANCE CHARACTERISTICS

7a) Productivity	Mediocre productivity	Fair to good productivity	Good productivity	Excellent productivity
7b) Excessive absence and turnover	Tends to be high when people are free to move	Moderately high when people are free to move	Moderate	Low

Source: *New Patterns of Management*, R. Likert (McGraw-Hill Book Company).

Appendix 7   Aide memoire used to interview specialists

THE DEVELOPMENT OF SPECIALISTS IN
THE PROBATION SERVICE

Interview aide memoire

1. How did your specialism come about?

2. How do you feel about your work?

3. To whom do you feel accountable?

4. What support systems exist?

5. On what basis are you specialising?
   (e.g. secondment/permanent/informal team/legitimate team/by task/by method/client need/type of client)

6. What are your professional development and training needs?

7. a) Is your task to be evaluated?

   b) How could your task be evaluated?

Appendix 8 Results of Likert questionnaire

ORGANIZATIONAL AND PERFORMANCE CHARACTERISTICS OF DIFFERENT MANAGEMENT SYSTEMS BASED ON A COMPARATIVE ANALYSIS

Opening characteristics	SYSTEM OF ORGANIZATION			
	Authoritative		Participative	
	Exploitive authoritative	Benevolent authoritative	Consultative	Participative group
1 CHARACTER OF MOTIVATIONAL FORCES				
1a) Underlying motives tapped	—	1	5	2
1b) Manner in which motives are used	—	—	7	2
1c) Satisfaction derived	1	4	4	—
2 CHARACTER OF COMMUNICATION PROCESS				
2a) Amount of interaction and communication aimed at achieving organization's objectives	1	3	5	—
2b) Direction of information flow	1	4	3	1

| | SYSTEM OF ORGANIZATION | | | |
| | Authoritative | | Participative | |
Operating characteristics	Exploitive authoritative	Benevolent authoritative	Consultative	Participative group
2c) Downward communication				
1) Where initiated	1	4	3	1
2) Extent to which communications are accepted by subordinates	2	1	5	1
2d) Upward communication				
1) Adequacy of upward communication via line organization	—	4	5	—
2) Subordinates' feeling of responsibility for initiating accurate upward communication	—	3	3	3
3) Forces leading to accurate or distorted information	—	4	2	3
4) Accuracy of upward communication via line	1	2	4	2

3 CHARACTER OF INTERACTION — INFLUENCE PROCESS

3a) Amount and character of interaction	—	4	5	—

3b) Amount of cooperative teamwork present	1	—	7	1
3c) Extent to which sub-ordinates can influence the goals, methods and activity of their units and depts				
1) As seen by superiors	—	2	4	2
2) As seen by sub-ordinates	1	2	5	1

4 CHARACTER OF DECISION-MAKING PROCESS

4a) At what level in organization are decisions formally made?	3	2	4	—
4b) Extent to which technical and pro-fessional knowledge is used in decision making	1	5	3	—
4c) Is decision making based on man-to-man or group pattern of operation? Does it en-courage or discourage teamwork?	—	2	7	—

5 CHARACTER OF GOAL-SETTING OR ORDERING

5a) Manner in which usually done	—	7	2	—

Operating characteristics	SYSTEM OF ORGANIZATION			
	Authoritative		Participative	
	Exploitive authoritative	Benevolent authoritative	Consultative	Participative group

6 *CHARACTER OF CONTROL PROCESSES*

6a) Extent to which the review and control functions are concentrated	—	8	1	—

7 *PERFORMANCE CHARACTERISTICS*

7a) Productivity	—	6	3	—
7b) Excessive absence and turnover	—	2	3	4

Source: *New Patterns of Management*, R. Likert (McGraw-Hill Book Company).

Appendix 9 Check lists used on South West Regional Staff Development Unit, on new managers' courses

CHECK LIST FOR ACHIEVING THE TASK:

Am I clear about my own responsibilities and my own authority?

Am I clear about the objectives of my group now and for the next few years (months) and have I agreed them with my supervisor?

Have I worked out a programme for reaching these objectives?

Can the job be restructured to get better results?

Are the physical working conditions (e.g. layout, equipment, lighting) right for the job?

Does everyone know to whom they are accountable?

Is the line of authority clear?

Are there any gaps in the abilities of the group (including mine) necessary to complete the task? If so, am I taking steps to fill them by training, by additional staff or the use of specialists?

Am I aware just how I and my group are spending our time? Is it the best way? Are our priorities right?

On those occasions when I am directly involved with the 'technical' work, do I make arrangements so that the needs of the group and its members are not ignored or overlooked?

Do I receive regular records which enable me to check progress and to pinpoint weaknesses and deviations?

What arrangements do I make for continuity of leadership in my absence?

Do I periodically take stock? Have I achieved the tasks set 12 months ago? If not, why not?

Do my work and behaviour standards set the best possible example to the group?

INDIVIDUAL NEED

If the needs of the individual are to be satisfied at work they:

- Must feel a sense of personal achievement in the job they are doing, that they are making a worthwhile contribution to the objectives of the group or section;
- Must feel that the job itself is demanding their best;
- Must receive adequate recognition for their achievements;
- Must feel secure within the terms of reference;
- Must have control over those aspects of their job which have been delegated to them;
- Must feel that they as individuals are developing, that they are advancing in experience and ability.

To provide the right 'climate' and the opportunities for these needs to be met for each individual in the group is probably the most difficult but certainly the most challenging and rewarding task of the leader.

CHECK LIST FOR MEETING INDIVIDUAL'S NEEDS

For each member of the group:

Have I agreed with each of my subordinates his main responsibilities (expressed as results) and standards of performance by which we can both recognise success?

Have they a continuing list of agreed short-term targets for the improvement of their performance each with its agreed maturity date?

Do they have the resources necessary to achieve the agreed performance standards (including sufficient authority)?

Have I made adequate provision for the training and (where necessary) retraining of each person?

In the event of success, do I acknowledge it and build on it? In the case of failure, do I criticise constructively and give guidance on improving future performance?

Does the individual see some pattern of career (and salary) development (unless, perhaps they are about to retire; in which case do they need help in meeting the problems of retirement)?

Can I remove some controls, though still retaining my accountability? E.g. can I cut down the amount of checking I do, holding them responsible more and more for the quality and accuracy of their work?

Am I sure that, for each individual work, capacity and pay are in balance?

If after opportunities for training and development they are still not meeting the requirements of the job, do I try and find a position for them more nearly matching their capacity — or see that someone else does?

Do I know enough about each member of the group to enable me to have an accurate picture of their needs, aptitudes and attitudes within the working situation?

Do I give sufficient time and personal attention to matters of direct concern to the individual, such as superannuation and redundancy arrangements, and where relevant, social and recreational opportunities?

GROUP NEED

Although we are employed on the basis of individual contracts, it is in groups or teams that the majority of our work is conducted.

A group exists as an entity and, as with individuals, no two groups are alike. A group has power to set its own standards of behaviour and performance and to impose them even when contrary to the interest of the individual and the organisation.

The successful supervisor understands that a group has its own personality, its own power, its own attitudes, its own standards and its own needs. You achieve your success by taking these things into account. You have constantly to respond to the needs of the group. At times this means withdrawing from your position 'way out front' and concentrating on 'serving those who serve him'. On these occasions you must be prepared to represent the group and speak with its voice. At the same time avoid 'over-identifying' with the group.

The key functions of the leader in meeting group needs are:

- To set and maintain group objectives and group standards;
- To involve the group as a whole in the achievement of objectives;
- To maintain the unity of the group and to see that dissident activity is minimised.

CHECK LIST FOR MEETING GROUP NEEDS

Do I set group objectives with the members and make sure that everyone understands them?

Is the group clear as to the working standards expected from them, e.g. in timekeeping, quality of work, housekeeping, safety? Am I fair and impartial in enforcing them? Is the group aware of the consequences of infringement (penalties)? Do I and the group understand the discipline procedure?

Is the size of working groups correct and are the right people working together? Is there a need for sub groups to be constituted?

Do I look for opportunities for building teamwork into jobs?

Do I take action on matters likely to disrupt the group, e.g. unjustified differentials in pay, uneven work loads, discrepancies in the distribution of overtime?

Is there a formal and fair grievance procedure understood by all? Do I deal with grievances and complaints properly?

Do I welcome and encourage new ideas and suggestions from the group?

Do I provide regular opportunities for genuine consultation of the group before taking decisions affecting them, e.g. decisions relating to work plans and output, work methods and standards?

Do I regularly brief the group on the organisation's current plans and future developments?

Do I accept the valuable part trade unions can play in the formal system of representation? Do I encourage members of the group

194

to be active members of unions or other representation bodies?

Am I prepared to 'go in to bat' for the group when this is required?

MANAGER'S CHECK LIST

Accept responsibility;

Work effectively;

Make sure your team knows its objective(s);

Make sure all people understand their jobs;

Have team meetings and listen;

Let higher management know what is happening (hopes, fears and expectations);

Have on the job training plan;

Face up to the problems before they become issues;

Walk the job every day;

Be fair, be honest, be loyal, be consistent.

Bibliography

Adair, John (1983), *Effective Leadership (A Modern Guide to Developing Leadership Skills)*, Pan Books (Business Management).

Adams, Sheena, Moss, Les and Pleasance, Geoff (1980), 'Who makes policy. How and why?', *Probation Journal*, vol. 27, no. 4, December.

Ainley and Kingstone (1981), 'Live supervision in a probation setting', *Social Work Education, 1*.

Baird Committee Report (1920).

Blau, P.M. and Scott, R.W. (1966), *Formal Organisations*, Routledge Paperback.

Bochel, Dorothy (1976), *Probation and After Care Service*, Scottish Academic Press.

Booth, T., Martin, D. and Melotte, C. (1980), *Specialisation: Issues in the Organisation of Social Work*, BASW Publication.

Brearly, Paul (1982), *Risk and Social Work*, Routledge and Kegan Paul.

Brieland, Briggs and Leuenberger (n.d.), *The Team Model of Social Work Practice*.

Brown, A. (1984), *Consultation: An Aid to Successful Social Work*.

Brunel Institute of Organisation and Social Studies (1978), *Developing Patterns of Work and Organisation*.

Butterworth Report (1972), HMSO, Cmnd 5076.

Byrne, P.S. (1973), *Learning to Care, Person to Person*, Churchill, Livingstone.

Clarke, F. and Arkava, M.L. (1979), *The Pursuit of Competence in Social Work*, Jossey Bass.

Cohen, Fink, Gaddon and Willits (1975), *Effective Behaviour in Organisations*, Irwin.

Cohen, Yona (1976), 'Staff supervision in probation', *Federal Probation*, September.

Collins, S.A. (1973), 'A study of the formal individual supervision of main grade probation staff in the probation service', unpublished.

Criminal Justice Bill (1925).

Danbury, Hazel (1979), *Teaching Practical Social Work*, Bedford Square Press.

DHSS Report (1974), *Social Service Teams — The Practitioner View*, HMSO.

Duncan, P.K. (1982), *Current Topics in Organisational Behaviour Management*, Haworth Press.

East Midlands Probation Services (1986), *Staff Supervision: Care and Control?*, NAPO.

Edelwich, Jerry (1980), *Burn-Out*, Human Science Press.

Etzioni, A. (ed.) (n.d.), *The Semi Professionals and their Organisations*, p. 142.

Fielding, Nigel (1984), *Probation Practice*, Aldershot: Gower.

Forder, A. (1966), *Social Casework and Administrator*, Faber and Faber.

Foren, Robert (1977), *Casework Supervision in the PACS*.

Glastonbry, Bryan (1980), *Social Work in Conflict*, London: Croom Helm.

Gorman, Joanne (1963), *Some Characteristics of Consultation*, New York: National Association of Social Workers.

Greater Manchester Probation Service (1980), *Priority Areas of Work in the Probation Service*.

Green, J. and Glanfield, P. (1983), '"Seniorless" teamwork with homeless clients', *Probation Journal*, vol. 30, no. 4.

Guise, Jenny (1985), *West Midlands Probation Service*, unpublished.

Guise, Jenny (1986), 'Staff supervision Working Party Discussion starter', unpublished.

Harman, J. (1976), 'A teamwork approach at IMPACT', *Social Work Today*, vol. 9, no. 36.

Haward, Christine (1979), *A Fair Assessment*, CCETSW.

Haxby, David (1978), *Probation*, Constable.

Heap, Elizabeth (1975), 'The supervision as reflector', *Social Work Today*, vol. 5, no. 22, 6 February.

Hey and Rowbotham (1975), *Task and Supervision in Area Social Work*.

Home Office (1977), *Probation and After-Care Service, Ethnic Minorities*, circular 113/77.

Home Office (1983), *Statement of National Aims and Objectives*.

Hughes, J.A. (1980), *The Philosophy of Social Research*, Longman.

Jarvis, F. (1972), *Advise, Assist and Befriend — A History of the Probation and After Care Service*, London: Butterworths.

Kadushin, A. (1976), *Supervision in Social Work*.

Kadushin, A. (1977), *Consultations in Social Work*, Columbia University Press.

Kast, F.E. and Rozenzweig, J.E. (1984), *Organisation and Management*, McGraw Hill.

King, J. (1958), *The Probation Service*, NAPO.

King, J. (1969), *The Probation and After Care Service*, Butterworths.

Kirkpatrick, J. (1980), 'The management structure review. A response', *Probation Journal*, vol. 27, no. 4, December.

Leeson, Cecil (1914), *The Probation System*, London: P.S. King & Son.

Lewis, Peter (1975), *Organisational Communications*, GRID Inc.

Lewis, Peter (1978), 'An approach to teamwork', *Social Work Today*, vol. 9, no. 36.

Lyons, K. (1984), *Team Leadership in a Patch System*, Social Work Monograph, published by University of East Anglia.

MacLaren, R. and Pieron, J. (1984), 'The ghost in the bureaucratic machine', *Community Care*, 24 May.

Maple, Frank (1977), *Shared Decision Making*, Sage Publications.

Marsh, J.W. (1980), 'A response to who makes policy: Why and how', *Probation Journal*, vol. 27, no. 4.

Marshall, M., Shoot, M. and Wincott, E. (1979), *Teamwork For and Against*, BASW.

Maslow, A. (n.d.), *Motivation and Personality*.

Mattinson, Janet (1975), *The Reflective Process in Casework Supervision*, Institution of Marital Studies.

McGregor, D. (n.d.), *The Human Side of Enterprise*.

Miles, Ieuan (1985), 'Professionalism and Social Work', unpublished.

Millard, D. (1978), 'Teamwork in probation. Prospects and implications', *Social Work Today*, vol. 9, no. 36.

Miller, E.J. and Rice, A.K. (1967), *Systems of Organisation*, Tavistock.

Monger, Mark (1972), *Casework in Probation*, Butterworths.

The Morison Report (1962), HMSO, Cmnd 1650.

Moser, C.A. and Kalton, G. (1979), *Survey Methods in Social Investigation*, HEB.

Mullen, E.J. and Dampson, J.R. (1976), *Evaluation of Social Intervention*, Jossey Bass.

Nadler, David (1981), *Feedback and Organisation Development Using Data Based Methods*, Addison Wesley Publishing Company.

NAPO (1980), 'The management structure review', *NAPO Newsletter*.

NAPO (East Midlands Branch) (1984), *Report of Working Party on Supervision*.

Obyrne, Patrick (1977), 'First line supervision in management theory. Is it the key to effectiveness?', *Social Work Today*.

Parsloe, Phylidda (1967), *The Work of the Probation and After-Care Officer*, Routledge and Kegan Paul.

Patrick, P. (1981), 'Officers mess — the management of the probation service', *Social Work Today*.

Payne, C. and Scott, A. (1982), *Developing Supervision of Teams in Field and Residential Social Work, Part 1*, National Institute of Social Work, paper no. 12.

Payne, M., *Working in Teams*.

Payne, M. (1979), *Teamwork For and Against. The Task of the Team Leader*.

Pettes, D.E. (1979), *Staff and Student Supervision*, George Allen and Unwin.

Probation Papers (1966), *Seniority in the Probation Service*, NAPO.

Probation Rules (1926).

Probation Rules (1949).

Raynor, P. (1984), 'National objectives and priorities: a comment', *Probation Journal*, vol. 31, no. 2.

Report of the Working Party on Management Structure in the Probation Service (1980).

Review of Social Work in Courts (1935).

Roberts, C. and Seddon, M. (1986), 'Staff Supervision Working Party Discussion Starter', unpublished.

Roberts, J. (1984), *Management, Innovation and Probation Practice*, NAPO.

Rowley, Josephine (1974), 'Trial and error', *Social Work Today*, vol. 5, no. 14.

Smith, Donna and Kingston, Philip, 'West Midlands Probation Service', unpublished.

Smith, Donna and Kingston, Philip (1983), *Basis for Live Consultation/Supervision*.

Stevenson, Parsloe, DHSS (1978), *Social Services Teams — Practitioners View*, chapter VIII on 'Supervision and accountability', DHSS.

Tibbert, J. (1969), 'Styles of Staff Supervision', unpublished.

Vickery, A. (1977), *Caseload Management — A Guide for Supervisors of Social Work Staff*, National Institute of Social Work Paper.

Watson, Kenneth (1973), 'Differential supervision', *Journal of Social Work*, November.

Weber, M. (1964), *The Theory of Social and Economic Organisation*, Free Press.

Westheimer, Ilse (1977), *The Practice of Supervision in Social Work*, Ward Lock Educational.

Wilkinson, Alan (1971), *Information for Managers*, Isaac Pitman and Sons.

Williamson, D.A. (1977), 'Perceptions of Staff Supervision in the Probation Service', West Yorkshire Probation Service, unpublished.

Willson, M.A. (1984), 'Management, retention and control of skilled, sophisticated staff in the late '80s', *Probation Journal*, vol. 31, no. 1, March.

Younghusband, E. (1978), *Social Work in Britain 1950-75, Volume 1*, George Allen and Unwin.

Index